# Introduction to Arduino

**A piece of cake!**

by Alan G. Smith

August 14, 2011

**Introduction to Arduino: A piece of cake!**

The author can be contacted at: alan@introtoarduino.com

ISBN: 1463698348
ISBN-13: 978-1463698348

This book is dedicated to:

My wife who first encouraged me to teach this class and then put up with my spending countless hours on this book and also helped with numerous comments on the first proof.

My children who excite me about teaching.

My father who spent many hours with me on the Vic 20, Commodore 64, and the robotic arm science project. Without his investment, I wouldn't be the engineer I am today.

All who would desire to make something, may this book help you with your inventions.

*Whatever you do, work at it with all your heart, as working for the Lord, not for men.*
*Colossians 3:23 (NIV 1984)*

# Contents

*Contents*

# Listings

*Listings*

# Chapter 1

# Getting Started

The purpose of this book is to get you started on the road to creating things using micro-controllers. We will discuss only enough electronics for you to make the circuits, and only enough programming for you to get started. The focus will be on your making things. It is my hope that as you go through this book you will be flooded with ideas of things that you can make. So let's get going...

The first question we'll start with is:

## 1.1 What is a Microcontroller?

Wikipedia[1] says:

> A micro-controller is a small computer on a single integrated circuit containing a processor core, memory, and programmable input/output peripherals

The important part for us is that a micro-controller contains the processor (which all computers have) and memory, and some input/output pins that you can control. (often called GPIO - General Purpose Input Output Pins).

---

[1] http://en.wikipedia.org/wiki/Microcontroller - 17 March 2011

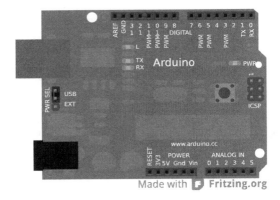

For this book, we will be using the Arduino Uno board. This combines a micro-controller along with all of the extras to make it easy for you to build and debug your projects.

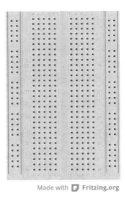

We will be using a breadboard in this book. This is a relatively easy way to make circuits quickly. Breadboards are made for doing quick experiments. They are not known for keeping circuits together for a long time. When you are ready to make a project that you want to stay around for a while, you should consider an alternative method such as wire-wrapping or soldering or even making a printed circuit board (PCB).

The first thing you should notice about the breadboard is all of the holes. These are broken up into 2 sets of columns and a set of rows (the rows are divided in the middle). The columns are named a, b, c, d, e, f, g, h, i, and j (from left to right). The rows are numbered 1 - 30. (from top to bottom). The columns on the edges do not have letters or numbers.

The columns on the edges are connected from top to bottom inside of the breadboard to make it easy to supply power and ground. (You can think of ground as the negative side of a battery and the power as the positive side.) For this book our power will be +5 volts.

Inside of the breadboard, the holes in each row are connected up to the break in the middle of the board. For Example: a1,b1,c1,d1,e1 all have a wire inside of the breadboard to connect them. Then f1, g1, h1, i1, and j1 are all connected. but a1 is not connected to f1. This may sound confusing now, but it will quickly come to make sense as we wire up circuits.

## 1.2 Install the Software

If you have access to the internet, there are step-by-step directions and the software available at: `http://arduino.cc/en/Main/Software`

Otherwise, the USB stick in your kit[2] has the software under the Software Directory. There are two directories under that. One is "Windows" and the other is "Mac OS X". If you are installing onto Linux, you will need to follow the directions at: `http://arduino.cc/en/Main/Software`

### 1.2.1 Windows Installations

1. Plug in your board via USB and wait for Windows to begin its driver installation process. After a few moments, the process will fail. (This is not unexpected.)

2. Click on the Start Menu, and open up the Control Panel.

3. While in the Control Panel, navigate to System and Security. Next, click on System. Once the System window is up, open the Device Manager.

---

[2]This book was originally written to go along with a class. If you have the book, but not the kit go to `http://www.introtoarduino.com` for more information and all of the source code in this book.

3

4. Look under Ports (COM & LPT). You should see an open port named "Arduino UNO (COMxx)".

5. Right click on the "Arduino UNO (COMxx)" port and choose the "Update Driver Software" option.

6. Next, choose the "Browse my computer for Driver software" option.

7. Finally, navigate to and select the Uno's driver file, named "ArduinoUNO.inf", located in the "Drivers" folder of the Arduino Software download (not the "FTDI USB Drivers" sub-directory).

8. Windows will finish up the driver installation from there.

9. Double-click the Arduino application.

10. Open the LED blink example sketch: File > Examples > 1.Basics > Blink

11. Select Arduino Uno under the Tools > Board menu.

12. Select your serial port (if you don't know which one, disconnect the UNO and the entry that disappears is the right one.)

13. Click the Upload button.

14. After the message "Done uploading" appears, you should see the "L" LED blinking once a second. (The "L" LED is on the Arduino directly behind the USB port.)

### 1.2.2 Mac Installation

1. Connect the board via USB.

2. Drag the Arduino application onto your hard drive.

3. When Network Preferences comes up, just click "Apply" (remember the /dev/tty/usb.)

4. Start the program.

5. Open the LED blink example sketch: File > Examples > 1.Basics > Blink

6. Select Arduino Uno under the Tools > Board menu.

7. Select your serial port (if you don't know which one, disconnect the UNO and the entry that disappears is the right one.)

8. Click the Upload button.

9. After the message "Done uploading" appears, you should see the "L" LED blinking once a second. (The "L" LED is on the Arduino directly behind the USB connection)

## 1.3 The Integrated Development Environment (IDE)

You use the Arduino IDE on your computer (picture following) to create, open, and change sketches (Arduino calls programs "sketches". We will use the two words interchangeably in this book.). Sketches define what the board will do. You can either use the buttons along the top of the IDE or the menu items.

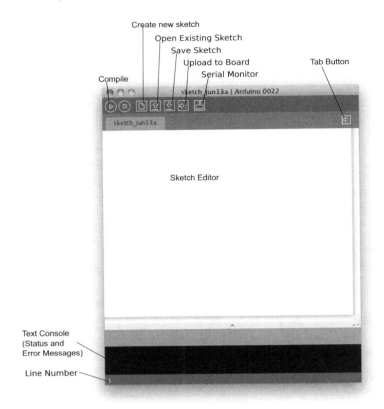

Parts of the IDE: (from left to right, top to bottom)

- Compile - Before your program "code" can be sent to the board, it needs to be converted into instructions that the board understands. This process is called *compiling*.

- Stop - This stops the compilation process. (I have never used this button and you probably won't have a need to either.)

- Create new Sketch - This opens a new window to create a new sketch.

- Open Existing Sketch - This loads a sketch from a file on your computer.

- Save Sketch - This saves the changes to the sketch you are working on.

- Upload to Board - This compiles and then transmits over the USB cable to your board.

- Serial Monitor - We will discuss this in section 5.1.

- Tab Button - This lets you create multiple files in your sketch. This is for more advanced programming than we will do in this class.

- Sketch Editor - This is where you write or edit sketches

- Text Console - This shows you what the IDE is currently doing and is also where error messages display if you make a mistake in typing your program. (often called a syntax error)

- Line Number - This shows you what line number your cursor is on. It is useful since the compiler gives error messages with a line number

## 1.4 Our first circuit

Before we get to the programming, let's connect an LED. LED stands for Light Emitting Diode. A diode only allows electricity to flow through it one way, so if you hook it up backwards it won't work.

If you connect the LED directly to power and ground, too much current will go through the diode and destroy it. To keep that from happening we will use a resistor to limit the current. You can think of a resistor like a water pipe. The higher the value of the resistor is like using a smaller pipe that lets less electricity "flow" through. This is not technically correct, but it is close enough for this book. We will use a 330 Ohm (Ohm is often shown as $\Omega$) resistor (Resistance is measured in ohms. Resistors have color bands on them that let you know what value they are.[3] A 330$\Omega$ resistor will have color bands: Orange-Orange-Brown) It doesn't matter which way you plug in a resistor.

The two leads (sometimes called "legs") of an LED are called an anode and a cathode. The anode is the longer lead. IMPORTANT: IF YOU PLUG IT IN

---

[3]We are not going to talk in this text about how to decide which size resistor to use.

BACKWARDS, IT WILL NOT WORK. (But it won't be damaged, either. Don't worry.)

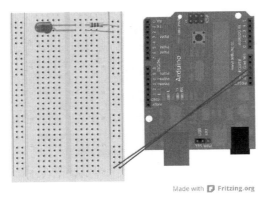

Made with Fritzing.org

1. With a wire, connect ground from the Arduino (labeled GND) to the bottom row of the farthest right column of the bread board.

2. With a wire, connect power from where it says 5V (the V stands for voltage and this is where the electric power comes from.) on the Arduino to the bottom row of the next to right column.

3. Connect the resistor with one end in h2 and the other end on the far right column (ground).

4. Connect the LED cathode (shorter leg) to f2. (This makes it connect to the resistor through the breadboard because they are on the same row.)

5. Connect the LED anode (longer leg) to f3.

6. Connect a wire from h3 to the next to right column (+5V).

7. Plug power into the Arduino .

8. The LED should light up. If it doesn't, unplug power from the Arduino, check all of your connections and make sure you have not plugged the LED in backwards. Then try power again.

Congratulations, you have made your first circuit!

## 1.5 Updated Circuit

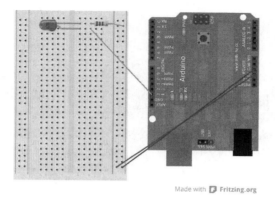

Made with **⬛ Fritzing.org**

Let's modify our circuit slightly so that the Arduino will be controlling the LED. Take the wire from h3 and connect it to pin 13 of the Arduino. You could use any pin, we are using pin 13 because the default program on the Arduino when you first get it blinks the "L" LED which is on pin 13 so we can check our circuit without any new software. (You should unplug your Arduino before making changes to the circuit. )

## 1.6 Our First Program

Now let's write a program to control the LED. Each program must contain at least two functions. A function is a series of programming statements that can be called by name.

1. *setup( )* which is called once when the program starts.

2. *loop( )* which is called repetitively over and over again as long as the Arduino has power.

So the shortest valid Arduino program (even though it does nothing) is:

Listing 1.1: Simplest Program

```
1  void setup()
```

```
2  {
3  }
4
5  void loop()
6  {
7  }
```

In most programming languages, you start with a program that simply prints "Hello, World" to the screen. The equivalent in the micro-controller world is getting a light to blink on and off. This is the simplest program we can write to show that everything is functioning correctly.

(Throughout this book we will show the program (sketch) in its entirety first, and then explain it afterwards. So if you see something that doesn't make sense, keep reading and hopefully it will be cleared up.)

Listing 1.2: led1/led1.pde

```
1   const int kPinLed = 13;
2
3   void setup()
4   {
5       pinMode(kPinLed, OUTPUT);
6   }
7
8   void loop()
9   {
10      digitalWrite(kPinLed, HIGH);
11      delay(500);
12      digitalWrite(kPinLed, LOW);
13      delay(500);
14  }
```

Here is a breakdown of what this program does.

```
1  const int kPinLed = 13;
```

This defines a constant that can be used throughout the program instead of its value. I **HIGHLY** encourage this for all pins as it makes it easy to change your software if you change your circuit. By convention, constants are named starting with the letter k. You don't have to do this, but it makes it easier when you look through your code to know what is a constant.

```
3  void setup()
4  {
5      pinMode(kPinLed, OUTPUT);
6  }
```

This sets up the pin that our LED is connected to as an OUTPUT pin. (Meaning that the Arduino is controlling "writing" to a pin instead of reading from it.)

```
8   void loop()
9   {
10      digitalWrite(kPinLed, HIGH);
11      delay(500);
12      digitalWrite(kPinLed, LOW);
13      delay(500);
14  }
```

These lines are where the action is. We start by writing HIGH out on the pin connected to the LED which will turn the LED on. (HIGH means putting 5V out on the pin. The other choice is LOW which means putting 0V out on the pin.)

We then call *delay( )* which delays the number of milliseconds ($\frac{1}{1000}$th of a second) sent to it. Since we send the number 500, it will delay for ½ second.

We then turn the LED off by writing LOW out on the pin.

We delay for 500 milliseconds (½ second)

This will continue until power is removed from the Arduino.

Before we go any further, try this on your Arduino and make sure it works. (there is an LED on the UNO board that is connected to pin 13 so if it blinks and your LED on the breadboard doesn't, then you probably put your LED in backwards.) You will know this works because this blinks the LED twice as fast as the original program that is on your Arduino. If it blinks once a second, then you have not successfully sent your new program to the Arduino.

## 1.7 Comments

So far our programs have been only for the computer. But it turns out that you can put things in them that are only for the human readers. You can (and should) add comments to the program which the computer ignores and are for human readers only. This language supports two forms of comments:

1. The block comment style. It starts with a /* and continues until a */ is encountered. This can cross multiple lines. Below are three examples.

```
/* This is a comment */

/* So is this */

/* And
 * this
 * as
 * well */
```

2. A single line comment. It starts with a // and tells the computer to ignore the rest of the line.

```
// This is also a comment
```

Here is an example of what our earlier program might look like with comments added:

(In this and all other code listings in this book, if a number doesn't show next to the line then it means it is a continuation of the line above but our paper isn't wide enough to show the entire thing. You will see an arrow at the end of the line that is to be continued and another arrow on the continuation line. That is just for this book, you will not see them in the IDE and you don't need to type them in.

Listing 1.3: Blink/Blink.pde

```
1  /*
2   * Program Name: Blink
```

12

```
3    * Author: Alan Smith
4    * Date Written: 17 March 2011
5    * Description:
6    *     Turns an LED on for one half second, then off for one ↩
         ↪ half second repeatedly.
7    */
8
9    /* Pin Definitions */
10   const int kPinLed =  13;
11
12   /*
13    * Function Name: setup
14    * Purpose: Run once when the system powers up.
15    */
16   void setup()
17   {
18       pinMode(kPinLed, OUTPUT);
19   }
20
21   /*
22    * Function name: loop
23    * Purpose: Runs over and over again, as long as the Arduino ↩
         ↪ has power
24    */
25   void loop()
26   {
27     digitalWrite(kPinLed, HIGH);
28     delay(500);
29     digitalWrite(kPinLed, LOW);
30     delay(500);
31   }
```

## 1.8 Gotchas

If your program won't compile (or it doesn't do what you expect), here are a few things to check that often confuse people:

- The programming language is case sensitive. In other words, *myVar* is different than *MyVar*

- Whitespace (spaces, tabs, blank lines) is all collapsed to the equivalent of a single space. It is for the human reader only.

- Blocks of code are encapsulated with curly braces ' *{* ' and ' *}* '

- Every open parenthesis ' *(* ' must have a matching close parenthesis ' *)* '

- Each program statement needs to end with a semicolon ' *;* '. In general, this means that each line of your program will have a semicolon. Exceptions are:
    - Semicolons (like everything) are ignored in comments
    - Semicolons are not used after the end curly brace.

## 1.9 Exercises

(There are sample solutions in Appendix C. However, you should struggle with them first and only look there when you are stuck. If you end up looking there, you should make up another exercise for yourself. The Challenge exercises do not have sample solutions.)

1. Change the amount of time the LED is off to 1 second. (Leaving the amount of time the LED is on at ½ second.)

2. Change the pin to which the LED is connected from pin 13 to pin 2. (Note that both the circuit AND the program must be changed.)

3. Hook up 8 LEDs to pins 2 through 9 (with resistors, of course.) Modify the code to turn on each one in order and then extinguish them in order. - HINT: hook them up one additional LED at a time and make sure the new one works before you add the next one.

4. CHALLENGE: Now that you have 8 LEDs working, make them turn on and off in a pattern different from the one in exercise 3.

# Chapter 2

# Making Light Patterns

## 2.1 "Blinky"

In the last chapter, we made a light blink. Now let's look into ways to vary the pattern for a single LED. (Later in the chapter we'll hook up even more LEDs.) We will use the LED that is built into our Arduino on pin 13 for the first few sections in this chapter. (It is labeled "L" on the board and is on the left side behind the USB connector.)

## 2.2 IF Statements

So far all of our programs have executed all of the code. Control structures allow you to change which code is executed and even to execute code multiple times.

The *if* statement is the first control structure. Here is an example of a program using it:

Listing 2.1: blink_if/blink_if.pde

```
1  const int kPinLed = 13;
2
3  void setup()
4  {
5      pinMode(kPinLed, OUTPUT);
6  }
7
8  int delayTime = 1000;
```

```
9
10  void loop()
11  {
12      delayTime = delayTime - 100;
13      if(delayTime <= 0){     // If the delay time is zero or ↵
                ↪ less, reset it.
14        delayTime = 1000;
15      }
16      digitalWrite(kPinLed, HIGH);
17      delay(delayTime);
18      digitalWrite(kPinLed, LOW);
19      delay(delayTime);
20  }
```

Can you guess what this program will do?

Let us go through it to make sure we all understand what it is doing and how to do similar things in our own programs.

Lines 1 - 7 are identical to our first program. The first change is in line 8.

```
8  int delayTime = 1000;
```

Notice that this is similar to line 1 except there is no *const* keyword. That is because this is not a constant. It is a variable (which means its value can change or vary during the program.) We give it a start value of 1000. (Variables that are defined within a set of curly braces can only be used within those curly braces. They are called "local" variables. Variables that are defined outside a set of curly braces (like this one) are "global" and can be used everywhere. )

Lines 9-11 are also identical to our first program, but then it starts to get very interesting.

```
12      delayTime = delayTime - 100;
```

Here we are changing the value of delayTime by subtracting 100 from its original value. Since the original value was 1000, after this happens the new value will be 900. Below are some of the math operators in the Arduino language.[1]

---

[1] The Arduino language is very closely related to C++. For more details, go to http://www. arduino.cc

| Operator[2] | Meaning |
|:---:|---|
| = | assignment operator |
| + | addition operator |
| − | subtraction operator |
| * | multiplication operator |
| / | division operator - be aware that if you are using integers only the whole part is kept. It is NOT rounded. For example: 5 / 2 == 2 |
| % | modulo operator - This gives the remainder. For example: 5 % 2 == 1 |

Next, we'll look at line 13-15:

```
13   if(delayTime <= 0){    // If the delay time is zero or ←
         ↪ less, reset it.
14      delayTime = 1000;
15   }
```

The purpose of this section is to make sure the light always blinks. Since we are subtracting 100 from delayTime, we want to keep it from becoming 0 or negative.

There are a number of comparison operators that we can use:

| Operator | Meaning |
|:---:|---|
| == | is equal to |
| != | is not equal to |
| < | is less than |
| > | is greater than |
| <= | is less than or equal to |
| >= | is greater than or equal to |

In this case, we could have just tested for *if(delayTime == 0)* but since being negative is bad as well, we checked for it. In general, this is a good practice. (Imagine if we wanted to subtract 300 from delayTime instead of 100.)

As you have probably figured out, if the delayTime is less than or equal to 0 then the delay time is set back to 1000.

---

[2]I am not mentioning all of the operators here, just the more common ones. A full list is in Appendix A.

```
16    digitalWrite(kPinLed, HIGH);
17    delay(delayTime);
18    digitalWrite(kPinLed, LOW);
19    delay(delayTime);
```

The remaining section turns the LED on and off. However, instead of using a fixed number, we use a variable so that we can change the delay time as the program runs. Pretty neat, huh?

## 2.3 ELSE Statements

An *if* statement can have an *else* clause which handles what should be done if the *if* statement isn't true. That sounds confusing, but here is an example:

Listing 2.2: blink_else/blink_else.pde

```
1  const int kPinLed = 13;
2
3  void setup()
4  {
5    pinMode(kPinLed, OUTPUT);
6  }
7
8  int delayTime = 1000;
9
10 void loop()
11 {
12   if(delayTime <= 100){   // If it is less than or equal to ←
         ↪ 100, reset it
13     delayTime = 1000;
14   }
15   else{
16     delayTime = delayTime - 100;
17   }
18   digitalWrite(kPinLed, HIGH);
19   delay(delayTime);
20   digitalWrite(kPinLed, LOW);
21   delay(delayTime);
```

18

```
22  }
```

As you have probably guessed already, the code in line 13 is only done if the delayTime is less than or equal to 100. Otherwise, the code in line 16 is done, but NEVER both. Only one or the other is done.

You may have noticed that instead of comparing to 0, like we did in section 2.2, that we compare to 100. This is because in this example we are comparing BEFORE we subtract 100 and in section 2.2, we compare AFTER.

A question for thought: What would happen if we compared to 0 instead of 100?

## 2.4  WHILE statements

A *while* statement is just like an *if* statement except it continues to repeat a block of code (a block of code is what is within the curly braces.) as long as the condition is true. (and there is no *else* statement) Perhaps an example will make this more clear:

Listing 2.3: blink_while/blink_while.pde

```
1  const int kPinLed = 13;
2
3  void setup()
4  {
5    pinMode(kPinLed, OUTPUT);
6  }
7
8  int delayTime = 1000;
9
10 void loop()
11 {
12   while(delayTime > 0){   // while delayTime is greater than 0
13     digitalWrite(kPinLed, HIGH);
14     delay(delayTime);
15     digitalWrite(kPinLed, LOW);
16     delay(delayTime);
17     delayTime = delayTime - 100;
```

```
18    }
19    while(delayTime < 1000){  // while delayTime is less than ←
         ↪ 1000
20      delayTime = delayTime + 100;   // do this first so we don←
           ↪ 't have a loop with delayTime = 0
21      digitalWrite(kPinLed, HIGH);
22      delay(delayTime);
23      digitalWrite(kPinLed, LOW);
24      delay(delayTime);
25    }
26  }
```

Can you figure out what this does?

Answer: It blinks faster, then slower.

## 2.5  What is truth(true)?

Ok, so there is something a little unusual about this programming language (which it shares with several others.) Rather than define what true is, it defines what false is and then defines everything as true that isn't false. This seems strange, but it works. *FALSE* is defined as zero (0). Everything else is defined as true. Sometimes you may come across code like this:

```
while (1){
    digitalWrite(kPinLed, HIGH);
    delay(100);
    digitalWrite(kPinLed, LOW);
    delay(100);
}
```

This will continue forever. [3] (Well, at least until you remove power or press the reset button on the Arduino.)

One of the side effects of this is one of the most common programming mistakes, accidentally using a = instead of a ==. Remember that a single equal

---

[3]There is an advanced programming statement called *break* that will get you out of a loop like this, but we don't cover it in this book.

sign = is an assignment (ie, it sets the variable to the value), and a double equals == is a test to see if they are the same.

For example, imagine if we wanted a light to blink in a speeding up pattern and then repeat but accidentally used a single equals instead of a double equals. We might have some code like this:

```
int delayTime = 1000;
void loop()
{
  if(delayTime = 0){   // BAD!!! should be ==
     delayTime = 1000;
  }
  digitalWrite(kPinLed, HIGH);
  delay(delayTime);
  digitalWrite(kPinLed, LOW);
  delay(delayTime);
  delayTime = delayTime - 100;
}
```

This will assign 0 to *delayTime*. The *if* statement will then check to see if 0 is true. It isn't (remember 0 is the definition of false.) So it doesn't execute the *delayTime = 1000*, but every time through the *loop()* function *delayTime* will be 0. This isn't what we wanted to have happen at all!!

For another example, imagine that we wanted the blinking to get less rapid and then reset but accidentally used a single equals instead of a double equals.

```
int delayTime = 100;
void loop()
{
  if(delayTime = 1000){   // BAD!!! should be ==
     delayTime = 100;
  }
  digitalWrite(kPinLed, HIGH);
  delay(delayTime);
  digitalWrite(kPinLed, LOW);
  delay(delayTime);
  delayTime = delayTime + 100;
}
```

In this case, it will assign 100 to *delayTime*. The *if* statement will then check to see if 100 is true. It is (remember everything that isn't 0 is true). So every time it will assign 1000 to *delayTime* and the blink rate will never change. Oops. These bugs can be difficult to track down so if you get something unusual look to make sure you didn't make this mistake.

## 2.6 Combinations

Sometimes you want to test for more than one thing. For example, you may want to test if a variable is between two numbers. While you can use multiple *if* statements, it is often more convenient and readable to use logical combinations. There are three ways that you can combine logical conditions.

| Operator | Example | Meaning |
|---|---|---|
| && | (A < 10) && (B > 5) | logical AND (return TRUE if condition A AND condition B are true, otherwise return FALSE.) |
| \|\| | (A < 10) \|\| (B > 5) | logical OR (return TRUE if condition A OR condition B is true, otherwise return FALSE.) |
| ! | !(A < 10) | logical NOT (return TRUE if condition A is false, otherwise return FALSE.) |

Something that isn't obvious is that you can use the NOT operator as a toggle for a variable that is intended to be either *true* or *false* (or *LOW* or *HIGH*). For example:

```
int ledState = LOW;

void loop()
{
    ledState = !ledState;    // toggle value of ledState
    digitalWrite(kPinLed, ledState);
    delay(1000);
}
```

In this case, *ledState* is LOW and then when *ledState = !ledState*, it becomes *HIGH*. On the next pass through the loop, *ledState* is *HIGH* and when *ledState = !ledState* it becomes *LOW*.

## 2.7 FOR statements

A *for* loop is the next control structure we will be talking about. It is most useful when you want something to happen some number of times. Here is a simple example.

Listing 2.4: blink_for/blink_for.pde

```
const int kPinLed = 9;

void setup()
{
  pinMode(kPinLed, OUTPUT);
}

void loop()
{
  for(int i = 0; i < 4; i++){
    digitalWrite(kPinLed, HIGH);
    delay(200);
    digitalWrite(kPinLed, LOW);
    delay(200);
  }
  delay(1000); // 1 second
}
```

There is something new in the *for* line above. What is the *i++*? Well, it turns out that programmers are a lazy bunch that don't like to type more than necessary. So they have come up with several shortcuts for commonly done things. These are called compound operators because they combine the assignment operator with another operator. All of the compound operators are listed in Appendix A.1.8. The two most common are:

| Operator | Meaning | Example |
|---|---|---|
| ++ | increment | *x++* means the same as *x = x + 1* |
| -- | decrement | *x--* means the same as *x = x - 1* |

The *for* statement has three sub-statements within it. It is composed like the following:

```
for (statement1;condition;statement2){
  // statements
}
```

Statement1 happens first and exactly once. Each time through the loop, the condition is tested; if it's true, the code within the curly braces and then the statement2 is executed. When the condition is false, it goes to the code after the statement block.

## 2.8 Our New Circuit

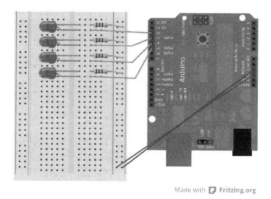

Made with 🗲 Fritzing.org

Ok, so now it is time to hook up more LEDs so we can do more exciting patterns.

1. Connect ground from the Arduino to the bottom row of the farthest right column.

2. Connect +5V from the Arduino to the bottom row of the next to right column. (This isn't actually necessary, but it is a good habit to always hook up the power and ground columns.)

3. LED1

   a) Connect the resistor with one end in h2 and the other end on the far right column (ground).

   b) Connect an LED cathode (shorter leg) to f2. (This makes it connect to the resistor through the breadboard.)

   c) Connect same LED anode (longer leg) to f3.

   d) Connect j3 to pin 2 on the Arduino.

4. LED2

   a) Connect another resistor with one end in h5 and the other end on the far right column (ground).

   b) Connect another LED cathode (shorter leg) to f5.

   c) Connect same LED anode (longer leg) to f6.

   d) Connect j6 to pin 3 on the Arduino.

5. LED3

   a) Connect another resistor with one end in h8 and the other end on the far right column (ground).

   b) Connect another LED cathode (shorter leg) to f8.

   c) Connect same LED anode (longer leg) to f9.

   d) Connect j9 to pin 4 on the Arduino.

6. LED4

   a) Connect another resistor with one end in h11 and the other end on the far right column (ground).

   b) Connect another LED cathode (shorter leg) to f11.

c) Connect same LED anode (longer leg) to f12.

d) Connect j12 to pin 5 on the Arduino.

Now, lets try a program that will let us make sure that all of our hardware is made correctly. It is often wise to write a small piece of software to test and make sure your hardware is correct rather than try your full software on the brand new hardware.

This code sets up LEDs on pins 2-5 and then cycles through turning each LED on and then off.

Listing 2.5: lightPattern1/lightPattern1.pde

```
1  const int kPinLed1 =  2;
2  const int kPinLed2 =  3;
3  const int kPinLed3 =  4;
4  const int kPinLed4 =  5;
5
6  void setup()
7  {
8    pinMode(kPinLed1, OUTPUT);
9    pinMode(kPinLed2, OUTPUT);
10   pinMode(kPinLed3, OUTPUT);
11   pinMode(kPinLed4, OUTPUT);
12 }
13
14 void loop()
15 {
16   // turn on each of the LEDs in order
17   digitalWrite(kPinLed1, HIGH);
18   delay(100);
19   digitalWrite(kPinLed2, HIGH);
20   delay(100);
21   digitalWrite(kPinLed3, HIGH);
22   delay(100);
23   digitalWrite(kPinLed4, HIGH);
24   delay(100);
25
26   // turn off each of the LEDs in order
27   digitalWrite(kPinLed1, LOW);
```

```
28    delay(100);
29    digitalWrite(kPinLed2, LOW);
30    delay(100);
31    digitalWrite(kPinLed3, LOW);
32    delay(100);
33    digitalWrite(kPinLed4, LOW);
34  }
```

While this code works just fine, it isn't very elegant and it seems like there is a lot of writing of very similar things and opportunities for mistakes. Let's see how we can do a better job.

## 2.9 Introducing Arrays

An array is a collection of variables that are indexed with an index number. An example will help us to understand.

Listing 2.6: lightPattern1b/lightPattern1b.pde

```
1   const int k_numLEDs = 4;
2   const int kPinLeds[k_numLEDs] =  {2,3,4,5}; // LEDs connected↩
        ↪  to pins 2-5
3
4   void setup()
5   {
6     for(int i = 0; i < k_numLEDs; i++){
7       pinMode(kPinLeds[i], OUTPUT);
8     }
9   }
10
11  void loop()
12  {
13    for(int i = 0; i < k_numLEDs; i++){
14      digitalWrite(kPinLeds[i], HIGH);
15      delay(100);
16    }
17    for(int i = k_numLEDs - 1; i >= 0; i--){
```

```
18    digitalWrite(kPinLeds[i], LOW);
19    delay(100);
20  }
21 }
```

Can you figure out what this does? If not, don't panic. We are going to go through this code and look at each part.

```
1 const int k_numLEDs = 4;
```

First, we define how many elements are going to be in our array. We use this later to make sure that we don't try to read (or write) past the end of our array. (Arduino does not stop you from doing this which can cause all sorts of strange problems.)

```
2 const int kPinLeds[k_numLEDs] =  {2,3,4,5}; // LEDs connected↩
    ↪  to pins 2-5
```

Second, we define the array. You'll notice that we have the number of "elements" in the array in brackets. We could have used the actual number, but it is much better to use a constant. We assign the values to the array here. The values are inside of curly braces and are separated by commas.

Arrays are zero-indexed, which can be confusing. That means the first element in the array *k_LEDPins* is *k_LEDPins[0]*. The last element in the array is *k_LEDPins[3]*. (0-3 is 4 elements.)

```
4 void setup()
5 {
6   for(int i = 0; i < k_numLEDs; i++){
7     pinMode(kPinLeds[i], OUTPUT);
8   }
9 }
```

Here we use a for loop to go through each of the elements in our array and set them as *OUTPUT*. To access each element in the array, we use square brackets with the index inside. [4]

---

[4]Some of you may be wondering if we could have just used pins 2-5 without using an array. Yes, we could have. But you don't want to. If in a later circuit you decide to use pins that aren't next to each other the array method works, and the other one doesn't.

```
13    for(int i = 0; i < k_numLEDs; i++){
14       digitalWrite(kPinLeds[i], HIGH);
15       delay(100);
16    }
```

This looks almost exactly the same as what is done in setup. Here we are going through each of the LEDs and turning them on (with a 100 millisecond delay in between them).

```
17    for(int i = k_numLEDs - 1; i >= 0; i--){
18       digitalWrite(kPinLeds[i], LOW);
19       delay(100);
20    }
```

Now we are showing that we can use a *for* loop to go backwards through the loop as well. We start at *k_numLEDs - 1* since arrays are zero-indexed. If we started at *k_LEDPins[4]*, that would be past the end of our array. We check *>= 0* since we don't want to miss the first element (the one at index 0.)

## 2.10 Exercises

1. Modify the blink_for program in Section 2.7 to light the LED up 10 times in a row instead of 4.

2. Make a program (sketch) that lights up a single LED five times in a row for one second on and off, and then five times in a row for ½ of a second on and off.

3. Make a program using arrays that lights up the LEDs from top to bottom and then goes backwards so only one LED is on at any time. (This is often called a "Cylon"[5] or a "Larson"[6] light.)

4. Make a program that lights up the LEDs in any pattern that you like.

---

[5]from Battlestar Galactica
[6]the producer of Knight Rider

# Chapter 3

# Input

Until now, we have only used the Arduino to control other things. It is time for us to start sensing the real world! After we do this, then our Arduino will be able to make decisions of what to do based off of input from the outside world.

In this chapter we will start with a simple circuit and continue to add pieces to it.

## 3.1 Pushbuttons

What is a pushbutton? Pushing a button causes wires under the button to be connected, allowing current to flow. (called closed) When the button isn't pressed, no current can flow because the wires aren't touching (called open) .[1]

The symbol for a pushbutton may be helpful here. You can tell that pushing down on the top causes there to be a connection, and a spring causes it to not be connected when it isn't being pushed down.

---

[1]This is true for the most common type of pushbutton called "normally open" (often abbreviated NO). There is a less common type called "normally closed" (abbreviated NC) that is closed (connected) when not pushed and open when pushed.

### 3.1.1 One button and an LED

### 3.1.1.1 Circuit

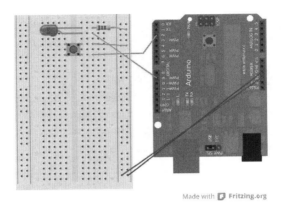

Made with 🟦 Fritzing.org

1. Connect the far right column (Ground) on the breadboard to GND on the Arduino.

2. Connect the next to right column (+) to 5V on the Arduino.

3. Put the pushbutton legs in e5, e7, f5, and f7. (If they won't fit in these squares, turn the switch 90° (¼ of a turn) and try again.)

4. Connect h7 to the pin 2 on the Arduino.

5. Connect h5 to the far right column (ground).

6. Connect a 330Ω (orange-orange-brown) resistor with one end in h2 and the other end on the far right column (ground).

7. Connect the LED cathode (shorter leg) to f2. (This makes it connect to the resistor through the breadboard.)

8. Connect the LED anode (longer leg) to f3.

9. Connect h3 to pin 9 on the Arduino.

The push buttons have four legs. When the button is pressed it connects the two legs on the right side together. (It also connects the two on the left, but we aren't using those now.)[2]

### 3.1.1.2 Programming

Let us start with some sample code and see if you can guess what it does.

Listing 3.1: button1/button1.pde

```
1  const int kPinButton1 = 2;
2  const int kPinLed = 9;
3
4  void setup()
5  {
6    pinMode(kPinButton1, INPUT);
7    digitalWrite(kPinButton1, HIGH); // turn on pull-up ←
          ↪ resistor
8    pinMode(kPinLed, OUTPUT);
9  }
10
11 void loop()
12 {
13   if(digitalRead(kPinButton1) == LOW){
14     digitalWrite(kPinLed, HIGH);
15   }
16   else{
17     digitalWrite(kPinLed, LOW);
18   }
19 }
```

Can you guess?

There are a number of things here that seem unusual, so let's talk about them.

```
4  void setup()
5  {
6    pinMode(kPinButton1, INPUT);
```

[2]Switches are rated by how much current and voltage can go through them. So don't try to replace the light switches in your house with these little buttons!

```
7   digitalWrite(kPinButton1, HIGH); // turn on pull-up ↩
        ↪ resistor
8   pinMode(kPinLed, OUTPUT);
9   }
```

First, we setup the buttonPin as *INPUT*. That is pretty straightforward.

Next, we write *HIGH* to the *INPUT* pin. Wait a second, how are we writing something to input?? Well, this is an unusual aspect to the Arduino. Writing *HIGH* to an input turns on an internal 20kΩ pull-up resistor. (Writing *LOW* to an input pin turns it off.)

The next obvious question should be "ok, what is a pull-up resistor?"

For electricity to flow, there has to be a complete circuit from the power to the ground. If a micro-controller pin is not connected to anything, it is said to be "floating" and you can't know ahead of time what the value will be when you read it. It can also change between times that it is read. When we add a pull-up resistor, we get a circuit like the following:

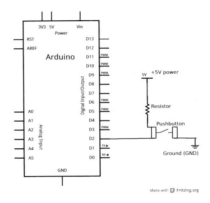

When a pushbutton is pushed down, the circuit is complete and ground is connected to pin 2. (The +5V goes through the closed switch to ground as well.) When it is not pushed down the circuit is from the +5V through the resistor and the micro-controller sees the +5V. (*HIGH*)

It turns out that this is so commonly needed that the designers of the Arduino put a resistor inside that you can use by writing some code. Isn't that neat?

Next, we look at our main loop:

34

```
11  void loop()
12  {
13    if(digitalRead(kPinButton1) == LOW){
14      digitalWrite(kPinLed, HIGH);
15    }
16    else{
17      digitalWrite(kPinLed, LOW);
18    }
19  }
```

If the button is pressed, then the pin will be connected to ground (which we will see as *LOW*). If it isn't pressed, the pull-up resistor will have it internally connected to +5V (which we will see as *HIGH*.)

Since we want the LED to light when the button is pressed, we write *HIGH* out when the value read from the pin connected to the button is *LOW*.

A few intermediate exercises:

1. Try this program and make sure it works. (If it doesn't, rotate the button 90 degrees and try again.)

2. Change it so the LED is normally on and pressing the button turns it off

### 3.1.2 Two buttons and an LED

Ok, so we could have done the last circuit without a micro-controller at all. (Can you figure out how to modify the first circuit in this book with a pushbutton to do the same thing?)

Now, lets do something a little more exciting. Let us make a circuit where we can change the brightness of an LED.

So far, we have either had the LED on (*HIGH*) or off (*LOW*).

How do we change the brightness of an LED?

It turns out there are two ways.

1. Change the amount of current going through the LED. (We could do this by changing the size of the resistor.)

2. Take advantage of the fact that people can only see things that happen up to a certain speed, and turn the LED on and off faster than we can see. The more time that the LED is on in a given period of time, the "brighter" we think it is. The more time it is off, the "dimmer" we think it is. (This method supports smoother dimming over a broader range as opposed to changing resistors.)

It turns out that this method of turning things on and off quickly is very common, and a standard method has been designed called Pulse Width Modulation (PWM for short).

The Arduino supports PWM (on certain pins marked with a tilde(~) on your board - pins 3, 4,5,9,10 and 11) at 500Hz. (500 times a second.) You can give it a value between 0 and 255. 0 means that it is never 5V. 255 means it is always 5V. To do this you make a call to `analogWrite()` with the value. The ratio of "ON" time to total time is called the "duty cycle". A PWM output that is ON half the time is said to have a duty cycle of 50%.

Below is an example showing what the pulses look like:

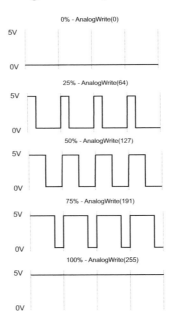

You can think of PWM as being on for $\frac{x}{255}$ where x is the value you send with `analogWrite()`.

### 3.1.2.1 Circuit

Enough talking! Let's make something! First, let us add to our circuit.

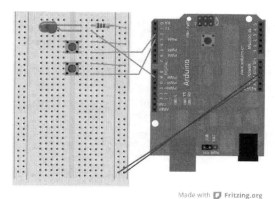

Made with ⬛ **Fritzing.org**

1. Place a second pushbutton in e9,e11,f9 and f11.

2. Connect h9 to the far left column (ground).

3. Connect h11 to pin 3 of the Arduino.

(You can test to make sure you have the button put in correctly by connecting h11 to pin 2 instead of the first button and making sure it works before you upload a new program to the Arduino.)

### 3.1.2.2 Programming

Here is a sample program that uses a button to dim the LED and another button to increase the brightness:

Listing 3.2: button2/button2.pde

```
const int kPinButton1 = 2;
```

```
2    const int kPinButton2 = 3;
3    const int kPinLed = 9;
4
5    void setup()
6    {
7      pinMode(kPinButton1, INPUT);
8      pinMode(kPinButton2, INPUT);
9      pinMode(kPinLed, OUTPUT);
10     digitalWrite(kPinButton1, HIGH); // turn on pullup resistor
11     digitalWrite(kPinButton2, HIGH); // turn on pullup resistor
12   }
13
14   int ledBrightness = 128;
15   void loop()
16   {
17     if(digitalRead(kPinButton1) == LOW){
18       ledBrightness--;
19     }
20     else if(digitalRead(kPinButton2) == LOW){
21        ledBrightness++;
22     }
23
24     ledBrightness = constrain(ledBrightness, 0, 255);
25     analogWrite(kPinLed, ledBrightness);
26     delay(20);
27   }
```

There are 3 lines that may need a little explaining

```
24     ledBrightness = constrain(ledBrightness, 0, 255);
25     analogWrite(kPinLed, ledBrightness);
26     delay(20);
```

Line 24 demonstrates a new built-in function that is very useful called *constrain()*. The function contains code similar to this:

Listing 3.3: Constrain

```
int constrain(int value, int min, int max)
{
```

```
    if(value > max){
        value = max;
    }
    if(value < min){
        value = min;
    }
    return value;
}
```

The functions we have written before all started with `void`, meaning they didn't return anything. This function starts with `int` meaning it returns an integer. (We will talk more about different types of variables later. For now, just remember that an integer has no fractional part.)

Ok, so what this means is line 24 guarantees the value of ledBrightness will be between 0 and 255 (including 0 and 255).

Line 25 uses analogWrite to tell Arduino to perform PWM on that pin with the set value.

Line 26 delays for 20 milliseconds so that we won't make adjustments faster than 50 times in a second. (You can adjust this to find where you think the best response is to your pressing the buttons.) The reason we do this is that people are much slower than the Arduino. If we didn't do this, then this program would appear that pressing the first button turns the LED off and pressing the second button turns it on (Try it and see!)

CHALLENGE question - What happens if both pushbuttons are pressed? Why?

## 3.2 Potentiometers

We used pushbuttons for digital input in the last section. Now let's look at using a potentiometer. (A potentiometer is a resistor whose value changes smoothly as it is turned. This is used often as an adjustment "knob" in many electronics.)

### 3.2.1 Circuit

The potentiometer has three legs. The one in the middle should be connected to ANALOG IN 0 on the Arduino. One of the sides should be connected to +5V and the other to GND. (ground). (If you get these backwards then your potentiometer will work in the backwards direction of what you expect.)

Digital means something is either on or off. Analog means it can have a continuous range of values. The Arduino has some built-in "analog inputs" that convert the voltage seen on the pin to a number that we can use in our programs. (They return between 0 and 1023. So, 0V would read as 0 and 5V would read as 1023.)

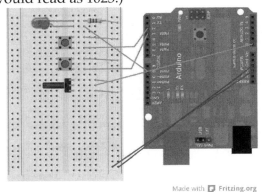

Made with **F** Fritzing.org

1. Place the potentiometer (often called "pot" for short) in f13, f14, and f15.

2. Connect j13 to the next to right most column (+5V).

3. Connect j15 to the right most column (ground).

4. Connect j14 to the A0 pin (Analog In 0) on the Arduino.

### 3.2.2 Programming

Listing 3.4: pot1/pot1.pde

```
const int kPinPot = A0;
const int kPinLed = 9;
```

```
3
4   void setup()
5   {
6     pinMode(kPinPot, INPUT);
7     pinMode(kPinLed, OUTPUT);
8   }
9
10  void loop()
11  {
12    int ledBrightness;
13    int sensorValue = 0;
14
15    sensorValue = analogRead(kPinPot);
16    ledBrightness = map(sensorValue, 0, 1023, 0, 255);
17
18    analogWrite(kPinLed, ledBrightness);
19  }
```

There are two things here that are different from anything we have done before.

1. The constant *k_PotPin* is defined as *A0*. (The A is a shortcut to mean it is one of the analog pins.)[3]

2. Line 16 demonstrates a new built-in function that is very useful called map(). This function re-maps a number from one range to the other. It is called like *map(value, fromLow, fromHigh, toLow, toHigh)*. This is useful because the analogRead returns a value in the range of 0-1023. But analogWrite can only take a value from 0-255. [4]

Since you can affect the brightness of an LED by varying the resistance, we could have just used the potentiometer as a variable resistor in the circuit. So

---

[3]Shhh, don't tell anyone but A0 actually means pin 14. A1 means pin 15, and so on. And you can actually use them as digital inputs and outputs if you run out of those pins. But you can't use digital pins as analog inputs. I recommend using the A# for the analog pins so it is obvious what you are doing.

[4]This maps linearly. So something that is halfway in the From range will return the value that is halfway in the To range.

now let us do something we can't do easily without a micro-controller. This next program changes how quickly the LED blinks based off of the value read from the potentiometer.

Listing 3.5: pot2/pot2.pde

```
const int kPinPot = A0;
const int kPinLed = 9;

void setup()
{
  pinMode(kPinLed, OUTPUT);
}

void loop()
{
  int sensorValue;

  sensorValue = analogRead(kPinPot);

  digitalWrite(kPinLed, HIGH);
  delay(sensorValue);
  digitalWrite(kPinLed, LOW);
  delay(sensorValue);
}
```

### 3.2.3 A way to avoid delay()

The program in the last section was pretty neat, but the light has to go through a full cycle of on and off before it checks the potentiometer again. So when the delay is long it takes it a long time to notice that we have changed the potentiometer. With some tricky programming, we can check the value more often and not wait until the full delay time was used up. Let's see an example.

Listing 3.6: pot3/pot3.pde

```
const int kPinPot = A0;
const int kPinLed = 9;

```

```
 4  void setup()
 5  {
 6    pinMode(kPinLed, OUTPUT);
 7  }
 8
 9  long lastTime = 0;
10  int ledValue = LOW;
11
12  void loop()
13  {
14    int sensorValue;
15
16    sensorValue = analogRead(kPinPot);
17    if(millis() > lastTime + sensorValue){
18      if(ledValue == LOW){
19        ledValue = HIGH;
20      }
21      else{
22        ledValue = LOW;
23      }
24      lastTime = millis();
25      digitalWrite(kPinLed, ledValue);
26    }
27  }
```

Let's talk about some things that are different.

```
 9  long lastTime = 0;
```

So far we have only used a variable type called *int*. It turns out that there are several different types of variables you can have. Here they are:

| Type | contains |
|---|---|
| *boolean* | can contain either true or false |
| *char* | -128 to 127 |
| *unsigned char* | 0 to 255 |
| *byte* | (same as unsigned char) |
| *int* | -32,768 to 32,767 |
| *unsigned int* | 0 to 65,535 |
| *word* | (same as unsigned int) |
| *long* (or *long int*) | -2,147,483,648 to 2,147,483,647 |
| *unsigned long* | 0 to 4,294,967,295 |
| *float* | -3.4028235E+38 to 3.4028235E+38 |
| *double* | (same as float) |

The only thing you need to know about this now is that if you are trying to store a number that may be too big to fit into an *int*, you can use a *long* (or a *long int*). (This table is true for Arduino, but can vary from computer to computer.)

The second new thing is that we are using a new function called *millis()*. This returns the number of milliseconds the Arduino has been running since it started last.[5] This function returns a *long* since if it returned an *int*, it wouldn't be able to count very long. Can you figure out how long? (Answer: 32.767 seconds)

## 3.3 RGB LEDs

Up until this point, we have used LEDs that are only a single color. We could change the color by changing the LED. Wouldn't it be cool if we could choose any color we wanted? What about teal, purple, orange, or even more???

Introducing our new friend, the RGB LED. An RGB LED is really three small LEDs next to each other. A Red one, a Green one, and a Blue one. (Hence, why it is called RGB). It turns out that you can make any color by mixing these three light colors together.

---

[5]It will actually "rollover" and start counting over again after about 50 days from when it is zero. But that is long enough it won't be important to you for this class.

You use the same PWM method we discussed earlier in the chapter for each part of the red, the green, and the blue. Let's hook it up with three potentiometers so we can vary each one and it should make more sense.

### 3.3.1 Circuit

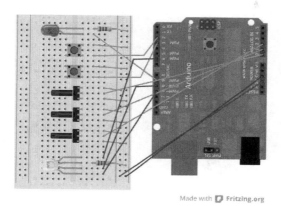

Made with **⬛ Fritzing.org**

This may look a lot more complicated, but it is all a repeat of other things you have done. You **CAN** do it!!!

1. Put a second Pot in f17, f18, f19. (The blue pots we are using for the class will be touching. This is ok.)

2. Connect j17 to the next to right most column (+5V).

3. Connect j19 to the right most column (ground).

4. Connect j18 to the A1 pin on the Arduino.

5. Put the third Pot in f21, f22, f23.

6. Connect j21 to the next to right most column (+5V).

7. Connect j23 to the right most column (ground).

8. Connect j22 to the A1 pin on the Arduino.

9. Put the RGB LED (you can tell it because it's the one with four legs) in f26, f27, f28, f29 with the cathode (longest leg) in f27. (this should be the leg second from the top.)

10. Put a resistor from h27 to the far right column (ground).

11. Connect h26 to pin 6 on the Arduino.

12. Connect h28 to pin 10 on the Arduino.

13. Connect h29 to pin 11 on the Arduino.

### 3.3.2 Programming

Following is a program that will let us control the color of the LED by turning 3 different potentiometers. One will be read for the value of Red, one for the value of Green, and one for the value of Blue.

Listing 3.7: rgb_3pot/rgb_3pot.pde

```
1  const int kPinPot1 = A0;
2  const int kPinPot2 = A1;
3  const int kPinPot3 = A2;
4  const int kPinLed_R = 6;
5  const int kPinLed_G = 10;
6  const int kPinLed_B = 11;
7
8  void setup()
9  {
10    pinMode(kPinLed_R, OUTPUT);
11    pinMode(kPinLed_G, OUTPUT);
12    pinMode(kPinLed_B, OUTPUT);
13  }
14
15  void loop()
16  {
17    int potValue;
18    int ledValue;
19
```

```
                            1);
                       1023, 0, 255);
                       lue);

                       ot2);
                       1023, 0, 255);
                       Value);
27
28     potValue              Pot3);
29     ledValue = map(pot       0, 1023, 0, 255);
30     analogWrite(kPinLed_B, ledValue);
31  }
```

You may notice that when you turn all of the pots to full on that instead of white you get red. The reason for this is that the red LED is stronger than the other two. You can experiment with the values in the *map()* function before sending it to the red part of the LED so that it will be more balanced.

## 3.4 Exercises

1. Make the two push buttons a "gas" and "brake" button. The "gas" button should speed up the blinking rate of the LED, and the "brake" button should slow it down.

2. Change the speed at which the LED blinks based off of the value of the pot ONLY when the first button is pressed. (In other words, you can adjust the potentiometer, but it has no effect until you press the "ON" button)

3. CHALLENGE: Use the two buttons to store a "from" and a "to" color. When neither button is pressed, the RGB LED should fade smoothly from one color to the other and back.

4. CHALLENGE: Can you find out how long it is between the last statement in the loop() function and the first one?

# Chapter 4

# Sound

So far we have just been playing with lights. In this chapter, we will add making simple sounds and music. In order to make a sound, we turn the speaker on and off a certain number of times per second.

Specifically, middle A ( a musical note) is 440 Hz. (Hz is short for and is pronounced "Hertz" - the number of times (or cycles) per second.)

So all we need to do to play a middle A is to make a sound wave that cycles 440 times per second. We will approximate the sine wave with a square wave (those terms just describe the shape). In order to calculate how much time we need to have the speaker on for:

timeDelay = $\frac{1 \text{ second}}{2 * \text{toneFrequency}}$. This has a 2 in the denominator because half of the time is with the speaker on and half is with the speaker off.

timeDelay = $\frac{1 \text{ second}}{2 * 440}$

timeDelay = 1136 microSeconds (a microsecond is $\frac{1}{1,000,000}$th of a second.)

## 4.1 Our Circuit

First, let's hook up the speaker to pin 9. (The other pin of the speaker simply goes to ground.)

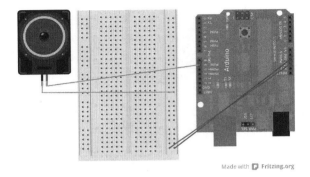

Made with 🄳 Fritzing.org

1. Connect the far right column (Ground) to GND on the Arduino.

2. Connect the next to right column (+) to 5V on the Arduino,

3. Connect the black wire of the speaker to the far right column (ground).

4. Connect the red wire of the speaker to pin 9 on the Arduino.

HINT: If the speaker is too loud,simply put a 330Ω resistor in between the speaker and pin 9 of the Arduino.

## 4.2 Simple note

We talked about the *delay()* function before. (Remember the units are in milliseconds or $\frac{1}{1000}$th of a second.) There is also a *delayMicroseconds()* function (a microsecond is $\frac{1}{1,000,000}$th of a second.)

So all we need to do is set up our speaker pin, and then raise and lower the voltage on that pin 440 times a second. Remember at the beginning of this chapter where we figured out that we need to have the speaker on (and then off) for 1136 microseconds.

Run this program and you should hear an A (musical note) that will not stop (until you pull power.)

Listing 4.1: sound_simple/sound_simple.pde

```
const int kPinSpeaker = 9;
```

```
2   const int k_timeDelay = 1136;
3
4   void setup()
5   {
6     pinMode(kPinSpeaker, OUTPUT);
7   }
8
9   void loop()
10  {
11    digitalWrite(kPinSpeaker, HIGH);
12    delayMicroseconds(k_timeDelay);
13    digitalWrite(kPinSpeaker, LOW);
14    delayMicroseconds(k_timeDelay);
15  }
```

## 4.3 Music

Now that we can make a simple note, we can make music.

It turns out that the Arduino has 2 functions built-in that handle making sounds as well.

The first is *tone()* which takes 2 required parameters (and an optional third).

*tone(pin, frequency, duration)*

OR

*tone(pin, frequency)*

These both return right away, regardless of the duration you give it. If you don't include a duration, the sound will play until you call *tone()* again or until you call *noTone()*. (This may require you using a delay function if playing a tone is the main thing you are doing.) The duration is in milliseconds.

The reason the duration is useful is that you can give it an amount of time to play and then you can go and do other things. When the duration is over it will stop.

The second is *noTone()* which takes a single parameter:

*noTone(pin)*

It basically stops whatever tone is playing on that pin.

(A strange warning. When the *tone( )* function is running, PWM (pulse width modulation that we used in section 3.1.2) won't run on pin 3 and pin 11. So if you are using a speaker in your sketch, you might want to avoid using those pins as PWM entirely.)[1] You may hook a speaker up to any of the pins.

Here is an example to try on your Arduino: (Ok, so it is a simple C scale and probably not really music.)

Listing 4.2: sound_2/sound_2.pde

```
#define NOTE_C4   262
#define NOTE_D4   294
#define NOTE_E4   330
#define NOTE_F4   349
#define NOTE_G4   392
#define NOTE_A4   440
#define NOTE_B4   494
#define NOTE_C5   523

const int kPinSpeaker = 9;

void setup()
{
  pinMode(kPinSpeaker, OUTPUT);
}

void loop()
{
  tone(kPinSpeaker, NOTE_C4, 500);
  delay(500);
  tone(kPinSpeaker, NOTE_D4, 500);
  delay(500);
  tone(kPinSpeaker, NOTE_E4, 500);
  delay(500);
  tone(kPinSpeaker, NOTE_F4, 500);
  delay(500);
  tone(kPinSpeaker, NOTE_G4, 500);
```

[1] I know you are probably curious about this really strange limitation. The details are beyond the scope of this book, so just remember the strange limitation.

```
28    delay(500);
29    tone(kPinSpeaker, NOTE_A4, 500);
30    delay(500);
31    tone(kPinSpeaker, NOTE_B4, 500);
32    delay(500);
33    tone(kPinSpeaker, NOTE_C5, 500);
34    delay(500);
35
36    noTone(kPinSpeaker);
37
38    delay(2000);
39  }
```

The only thing here you haven't seen before is *#define*. *#define* is a search and replace command to the computer during compilation. Any time it finds the first thing (up to a space), it replaces it with the rest of the line. [2] So in this example, when the computer finds *NOTE_E4*, it replaces it with a value of 330.

We won't talk here about how to determine what the frequency is of each note. However, there is a file on your USB stick called *pitches.h* that has all of the frequencies for all of the notes on a piano keyboard. This file is also available from `http://www.introtoarduino.com`.

## 4.4 Music with functions

It seems like there ought to be someway to reduce all of the repetition above. Up until this point, we have only used the two required functions or functions that come with the Arduino. It is time for us to create our own function!

Every function starts with what type of variable it returns. (*void* is a certain type that means it doesn't return anything.)

(Remember there is a list of variable types in Section 3.2.3. )

It then has the function name (how it is called), an open parenthesis " *(* " and then a list of parameters separated by commas. Each parameter has a variable type followed by a name. Then it has a close parenthesis " *)* ". The parameters

---

[2] These are called macros and you can actually do more powerful things with them but that is outside the scope of this book. If you are interested, do some searching on the internet.

can be used within the function as variables. As an example, we'll create a function called *ourTone()* that will combine the *tone()* and *delay()* lines so that the function won't return until the note is done playing.

Listing 4.3: sound_3/sound_3.pde

```
1   #define NOTE_C4   262
2   #define NOTE_D4   294
3   #define NOTE_E4   330
4   #define NOTE_F4   349
5   #define NOTE_G4   392
6   #define NOTE_A4   440
7   #define NOTE_B4   494
8   #define NOTE_C5   523
9
10  const int kPinSpeaker = 9;
11
12  void setup()
13  {
14    pinMode(kPinSpeaker, OUTPUT);
15  }
16
17  void loop()
18  {
19    ourTone(NOTE_C4, 500);
20    ourTone(NOTE_D4, 500);
21    ourTone(NOTE_E4, 500);
22    ourTone(NOTE_F4, 500);
23    ourTone(NOTE_G4, 500);
24    ourTone(NOTE_A4, 500);
25    ourTone(NOTE_B4, 500);
26    ourTone(NOTE_C5, 500);
27
28    noTone(kPinSpeaker);
29    delay(2000);
30  }
31
32  void ourTone(int freq, int duration)
33  {
```

54

```
34    tone(kPinSpeaker, freq, duration);
35    delay(duration);
36 }
```

Functions can be a huge help in making your program easier to understand.
Here is an example so we can now specify what we want to play in two
arrays (one that holds the notes, and one that holds the beats. )

Listing 4.4: sound_array/sound_array.pde

```
1  #include "pitches.h"
2
3  int kPinSpeaker = 9;
4
5  #define NUM_NOTES 15
6
7  const int notes[NUM_NOTES] = // a 0 represents a rest
8  {
9    NOTE_C4, NOTE_C4, NOTE_G4, NOTE_G4,
10   NOTE_A4, NOTE_A4, NOTE_G4, NOTE_F4,
11   NOTE_F4, NOTE_E4, NOTE_E4, NOTE_D4,
12   NOTE_D4, NOTE_C4, 0
13 };
14
15 const int beats[NUM_NOTES] = {
16   1, 1, 1, 1, 1, 1, 2, 1, 1, 1, 1, 1, 1, 2, 4 };
17 const int beat_length = 300;
18
19 void setup()
20 {
21   pinMode(kPinSpeaker, OUTPUT);
22 }
23
24 void loop()
25 {
26   for (int i = 0; i < NUM_NOTES; i++) {
27     if (notes[i] == 0) {
28       delay(beats[i] * beat_length); // rest
29     }
30     else {
```

```
31        ourTone(notes[i], beats[i] * beat_length);
32      }
33      // pause between notes
34      noTone(kPinSpeaker);
35      delay(beat_length / 2);
36    }
37  }
38
39  void ourTone(int freq, int duration)
40  {
41    tone(kPinSpeaker, freq, duration);
42    delay(duration);
43  }
```

In line 1, you'll see the *#include* statement. What this does is take the entire file within the quotes and put it where the *#include* statement is. By convention, these are almost always placed at the top of a program.

## 4.5 Exercises

1. Make a sketch that plays the first line of "Happy Birthday"

   a) C4 (1 beat), C4 (1 beat), D4 (2 beats), C4 (2 beats), F4 (2 beats), E4 (4 beats)

2. Add 2 buttons to the circuit. For a reminder of how to hookup and program buttons, see section 3.1. When you press each button have it play a different tune.

3. Change *ourTone()* to not use the *tone()* and *noTone()* functions. (HINT: use the technique shown in section 4.2.)

# Chapter 5

# Making a digital thermometer

Before we start on the fun work of making a digital thermometer, we are going to take a slight detour in the next section so that we can test out parts of our program before putting it all together. Writing small parts of your program and making sure it works before doing more is wise as it makes tracking down problems much much easier.

## 5.1 Serial Monitor

Until this point when our programs (sketches) didn't work, we just pulled out our hair and tried harder. Perhaps some of you put in an extra LED and turned it on and off at certain points in your program so that you would know what your program was doing.

Well, now we will learn a much easier way. Built into the Arduino platform is an ability to talk back to the user's computer. You may have noticed that Pins 0 and 1 on the Arduino say "RX" and "TX" next to them. These pins are monitored by another chip on the Arduino that converts these pins to go over the USB cable (if it is plugged in both to your Arduino and the computer.)

I have the entire program below first. Read through it, but we will explain the new parts after the sample program. This program is the same as the one in section 2.2 except it has some extra code in it to help us see what the program is doing.

Listing 5.1: blink_if_serial/blink_if_serial.pde

```
const int kPinLed = 13;

```

```
 3   void setup()
 4   {
 5       pinMode(kPinLed, OUTPUT);
 6       Serial.begin(9600);
 7   }
 8
 9   int delayTime = 1000;
10
11   void loop()
12   {
13       delayTime = delayTime - 100;
14       if(delayTime <= 0){    // If it would have been zero or ←
                ↪ less, reset it.
15         delayTime = 1000;
16       }
17       Serial.print("delayTime = ");
18       Serial.println(delayTime);
19       digitalWrite(kPinLed, HIGH);
20       delay(delayTime);
21       digitalWrite(kPinLed, LOW);
22       delay(delayTime);
23   }
```

You'll notice a couple of new things. First, there is a new line in the setup() function.

```
 6       Serial.begin(9600);
```

This basically says that we want to use the *Serial*[1] code and to start it at 9600 baud.[2] This number and the one in the serial monitor (described later) MUST match or you will see gibberish in the serial monitor. ( 9600 is the default, so it is easiest to use that.)

The second new thing is in lines 17-18.

```
17       Serial.print("delayTime = ");
18       Serial.println(delayTime);
```

---

[1]Serial means that it is sent one bit after another.
[2]Baud is how many bits per second are transmitted.

The only difference between *Serial.print* and *Serial.println* is that *Serial.println* means that the next thing sent out the serial port after this one will start on the next line. There is a third new thing you may have noticed. There is something in quotes ( " ). This is called a string. In this book we will only use strings as constants.[3]

Upload and run it. Hmm, it seems like the LED just blinked and nothing else new happened (except now we see the TX light blink on the board. That is because we don't have the Serial Monitor window up.

Open the Serial Monitor by clicking on the Serial Monitor box in the IDE. It should look like the screenshot below. Make SURE the baud (speed) is set to 9600. It is located in the bottom right corner. (The important thing is that it is set the same in our program and here. Since the default here is 9600, we set our

---

[3]A string is really an array of bytes. But a full discussion of strings is outside the scope of this book.

program to that to minimize our needing to change settings.) If you have the
baud set differently, you will see garbage instead of what you expect.

Before going any further, make sure that when you run your program you
see the lines "delayTime = " with the value of delayTime on the Serial Monitor.

## 5.2 Measuring the temperature

We are using a chip called TMP36. It can report the temperature from -40 degrees Celsius to 150 degrees Celsius (or -40 degrees Fahrenheit to 302 degrees
Fahrenheit.) Accuracy decreases after 125 degrees Celsius, but since water boils
at 100 degrees Celsius that is ok.

Here is a picture of the circuit:

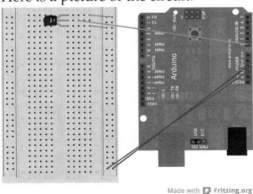

Made with **Fritzing.org**

1. Connect the far right column to ground (GND) on the Arduino.

2. Connect the next to right column to +5V.

3. Put pin 1 of the TMP36 in f1. (The curved part of the temperature sensor should face the left edge of the breadboard. If you get this backwards, it will heat up and can burn you.)

4. Connect j1 to the far right column (GND).

5. Connect j3 to the next to right column (+5V).

6. Connect j2 to A0 on the Arduino.

Now here is the code that will read the temperature sensor and send the values to the serial monitor on the computer. Again, we will show the entire code first and then go through the new sections afterwards.

Listing 5.2: temp_serial/temp_serial.pde

```
 1  const int kPinTemp = A0;
 2
 3  void setup()
 4  {
 5    Serial.begin(9600);
 6  }
 7
 8  void loop()
 9  {
10    float temperatureC = getTemperatureC();
11
12    Serial.print(temperatureC);
13    Serial.println(" degrees C");
14
15    // now convert to Fahrenheit
16    float temperatureF = convertToF(temperatureC);
17
18    Serial.print(temperatureF);
19    Serial.println(" degrees F");
20
21    delay(500);
22  }
```

```
23
24   float getTemperatureC()
25   {
26     int reading = analogRead(kPinTemp);
27
28     float voltage = (reading * 5.0) / 1024;
29     // convert from 10 mv per degree with 500mV offset
30     // to degrees ((voltage - 500mV) * 100)
31     return (voltage - 0.5) * 100;
32   }
33
34   float convertToF(float temperatureC)
35   {
36     return (temperatureC * 9.0 / 5.0) + 32.0;
37   }
```

So we'll start near the very beginning of loop.

```
10   float temperatureC = getTemperatureC();
```

You will notice that we use the *float* variable type. This variable type is the only one that allows you to store anything other than integer numbers (number with no decimal or fractional part.) Floats are only accurate to about 6-7 digits. This is important only because you can end up with rounding errors when using them. So when doing comparisons, make sure that you are checking to see if they are "close" instead of equal. We call our own function *getTemperatureC()*.

```
24   float getTemperatureC()
25   {
26     int reading = analogRead(kPinTemp);
27
28     float voltage = (reading * 5.0) / 1024;
29     // convert from 10 mv per degree with 500mV offset
30     // to degrees ((voltage - 500mV) * 100)
31     return (voltage - 0.5) * 100;
32   }
```

The *getTemperatureC* function does the math necessary to convert from the data the sensor gives into the Celsius temperature. Since our *analogIn()*

62

can return a value between 0 and 1023, we can calculate the voltage by multiplying our reading by 5.0 and dividing it by 1024. The sensor that we are using sends 500mV at 0 Celsius (so that you can read negative temperatures.) It then goes up 10mV per degree C. For example, here is what the sensor will return for some different temperatures.

| Temperature Celsius | Voltage from sensor |
|---|---|
| -10 | 400mV |
| 0 | 500mV |
| 10 | 600mV |
| 20 | 700mV |
| 30 | 800mV |
| 40 | 900mV |
| 50 | 1000mV |

This is the first function we have written that returns a value. (Remember, all of the other functions have been of type *void* meaning they don't return a value.) You will see that to return the value you simply put *return* followed by the value to return. (Instead of a value, you can put a calculation like we have done here.) Returning a value means that when you call a function it has an "answer" that you can assign to a variable.

We send that to the Serial Monitor and then we convert to Fahrenheit[4] by calling *convertToF( )*.

This function takes the temperature in Celsius and converts it to Fahrenheit. Converting from Fahrenheit to Celsius is the formula: $Fahrenheit = \frac{9}{5}(Celsius) + 32$

```
34  float convertToF(float temperatureC)
35  {
36      return (temperatureC * 9.0 / 5.0) + 32.0;
37  }
```

---

[4]Only 2 countries in the world STILL use Fahrenheit as the main temperature scale. The US and Belize.

## 5.3 Hooking up the LCD

LCD stands for Liquid Crystal Display. We will refer to it as either an LCD or simply a display.

There are a *large* number of different LCDs available. They come in all shapes and sizes. Some can display characters (letters and numbers) only and others can display graphics (pictures).

For this book, we are using an 84x48 graphical LCD. (That means that there are 84 pixels (dots) across and 48 pixels down.) Controlling an LCD directly would be very difficult, so most LCDs have a controller chip attached. This one has a PCD8544 for its controller.

In this chapter, we will just hook it up and use some routines to put text on the display. In the next chapter, we will explore what we can do a little more and put some graphics on the display as well.

You may have noticed that we have the LCD connected to a small PCB (printed circuit board) with another chip on it. That is because the LCD works at 3.3V and we are running the Arduino at 5V. The chip on the PCB does the voltage conversion for us so we won't damage the LCD.

There are 8 pins on the board. Here is a list of the pins and what they do:

| Pin | Description |
|-----|-------------|
| GND | This connects to Ground on the Arduino |
| 3.3V | Connect to the 3.3V power on the Arduino. This is power for the LCD. VERY important that this is connected to 3.3V and **NOT** 5V or you could damage the LCD. |
| CLK | The serial clock[5] |
| DIN | This is where the serial[6] data is sent |
| D/C | This lets the LCD know whether what is being sent to it is a command or data |
| CS | This is the Chip Select.[7] For this book, we will always tie it to GND |
| RST | This resets the controller on the LCD. |
| LED | Controls the backlight. We can connect it to +5V to be always on, or GND to be always off, or to a pin to be able to turn it on or off. [8] |

Now let's hook up the circuit.

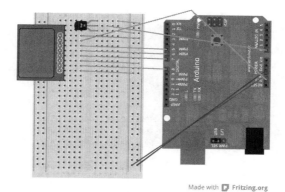

Made with **D** Fritzing.org

1. Place the LCD + PCB into the breadboard where the pins that are labeled

---

[5]The purpose of the serial clock is it lets the controller know when to look at DN for the next bit

[6]serial means it is sent one bit at a time

[7]When this is low then the chip is listening to D/C, DIN, CLK, and RST) This can either be tied to Ground (which will make it always listen) or used so that the pins can also be used for other purposes.

[8]Yes, we can even use PWM like we have earlier to have different brightness levels of the backlight.

on the purple PCB are in a4-a11.

2. Connect the far right column to GND on the Arduino.

3. Connect the next to right column to +5V on the Arduino.

4. Connect c4 to the far right column (ground).

5. Connect c5 to the 3V3 on the Arduino. (VERY IMPORTANT! DOUBLE CHECK before adding power.)

6. Connect c6 (CLK) to pin 5 on the Arduino.

7. Connect c7 (DIN) to pin 6 on the Arduino.

8. Connect c8 (D/C) to pin 7 on the Arduino.

9. Connect c9 (CS) to the far right column (ground). [9]

10. Connect c10 (RST) to pin 8 on the Arduino.

11. Connect c11 (LED) to the next to right column (+5V). This means that the backlight will always be on.

## 5.4 Talking to the LCD

While we could write all of the code to talk to the LCD, we are going to use some functions in a library. A library is a collection of code that can be used by multiple programs. This allows us to simply call functions that make it much easier to communicate with the LCD. If you are interested in how the LCD works, you can look inside the library but explaining that code is outside of the scope of this book.

---

[9]This means that the LCD will always be listening on its pins.

### 5.4.1 Installing the library

Create a directory called **libraries** within your **sketchbook** directory (Go to the Preferences menu item to see where your sketchbook directory is. Copy the files off the USB stick in the directory **/libraries** into the directory you just made.) If you don't have the USB stick, you can get the files from `http://www.introtoarduino.com` Then restart the Arduino IDE by quitting it and starting it over again. If you don't restart the Arduino IDE then you won't be able to use the library. The list of all of the functions in the library is in Appendix A.4.

### 5.4.2 Using the LCD

Like we have many times already, we will start with the whole program and then go through and discuss new parts.

Listing 5.3: lcd1/lcd1.pde

```
1  #include <PCD8544.h>
2
3  const int kPin_CLK = 5;
4  const int kPin_DIN = 6;
5  const int kPin_DC = 7;
6  const int kPin_RESET = 8;
7
8  PCD8544 lcd(kPin_CLK, kPin_DIN, kPin_DC, kPin_RESET);
9
10 void setup()
11 {
12   lcd.init();
13   lcd.setCursor(0,0);
14   lcd.print("Hello, World!");
15 }
16
17 void loop()
18 {
19   lcd.setCursor(0,1);
20   lcd.print(millis());
```

```
21  }
```

So, the first thing you will notice that is new is in line 1.

```
1  #include <PCD8544.h>
```

The *#include* tells the computer to take the file mentioned and when it is "compiling" the program to replace the *#include* statement with the contents of that file. An *#include* can either have the angle brackets which means to look in the library directory or it can have quotes which means to look in the same directory that the sketch is in.

The next few lines are our pin definitions. Then we create a variable of a new type.

```
8  PCD8544 lcd(kPin_CLK, kPin_DIN, kPin_DC, kPin_RESET);
```

In this statement we are defining a variable named lcd of type PCD8544[10] and telling the computer which pins are connected on the Arduino.

To define the variable we tell it what pin clk, din, dc, and reset are attached to.

```
10  void setup()
11  {
12    lcd.init();
13    lcd.setCursor(0,0);
14    lcd.print("Hello, World!");
15  }
```

In line 12, we call *lcd.init()* which will initialize the lcd. After this has returned, we can use the lcd.

In line 13, we set the cursor to the upper left of the screen. (There are 84 "columns" and 6 "lines" in this display. Just like in arrays, it starts at 0 instead of 1.)

In line 14, we print a message. This is very similar to how we sent messages over serial earlier in this chapter except we use lcd.print instead of serial.print.

---

[10]PCD8544 is the name of the LCD controller we are using. How to create new types of variables is outside the scope of this book but is a feature supported by the language.

```
17  void loop()
18  {
19    lcd.setCursor(0,1);
20    lcd.print(millis());
21  }
```

This is the code that is called over and over again.

In line 19, we set the cursor to the 0th column (far left), and the 1st row. (Remember that it starts at 0 so this is really the 2nd row.)

In line 20, we see a shortcut. We have used *millis()* before in section 3.2.3. We could have done this with 2 lines of code like:

```
long numMillis = millis();
lcd.print(numMillis);
```

However, in this case since we didn't need the value of the number of milliseconds for anything else, we just sent the result of the *millis()* function directly to *lcd.print()*.

## 5.5  Bringing it all together

So now, lets combine the thermometer code we did earlier in the chapter with the lcd code we just used.

Listing 5.4: temp_lcd/temp_lcd.pde

```
1   #include <PCD8544.h>
2
3   const int kPin_CLK = 5;
4   const int kPin_DIN = 6;
5   const int kPin_DC = 7;
6   const int kPin_RESET = 8;
7   const int kPin_Temp = A0;
8
9   PCD8544 lcd(kPin_CLK, kPin_DIN, kPin_DC, kPin_RESET);
10
11  void setup()
12  {
```

```
13    lcd.init();
14    lcd.setCursor(10,0);
15    lcd.print("Temperature:");
16  }
17
18  void loop()
19  {
20    float temperatureC = getTemperatureC();
21     // now convert to Fahrenheit
22    float temperatureF = convertToF(temperatureC);
23
24    lcd.setCursor(21,1);
25    lcd.print(temperatureC);
26    lcd.print(" C");
27    lcd.setCursor(21,2);
28    lcd.print(temperatureF);
29    lcd.print(" F");
30    delay(100);
31  }
32
33  float getTemperatureC()
34  {
35    int reading = analogRead(kPin_Temp);
36
37    float voltage = (reading * 5.0) / 1024;
38    // convert from 10 mv per degree with 500mV offset
39    // to degrees ((voltage - 500mV) * 100)
40    return (voltage - 0.5) * 100;
41  }
42
43  float convertToF(float temperatureC)
44  {
45      return (temperatureC * 9.0 / 5.0) + 32.0;
46  }
```

The only thing new and interesting in this program is that we used the *setCursor()* function to put the text mostly centered on the screen.

Congratulations, you now have a digital thermometer that reports the temperature in Celsius and Fahrenheit!

## 5.6 Exercises

1. Change the program so it displays the voltage returned from the sensor as well as the temperature in Celsius and Fahrenheit.

2. Change the program so it displays the temperature in Fahrenheit as well as the maximum and minimum temperatures it has seen.

3. CHALLENGE: Modify the program in exercise 2 to also show how long ago (in seconds) the minimum and maximum temperature were seen.

# Chapter 6

# Graphics (Pictures) on our LCD

Until this point, we have had just text on our LCD. However, we have a graphical LCD so it is time for us to draw some pictures on it. First, we will draw some static graphics (where we draw out what we want it to look like ahead of time). Then we will have the Arduino decide what to draw based off of input.

But before we can get to drawing, we'll need to take a quick detour to explain some details that will be necessary to send graphics to the display.

## 6.1  Binary and Hex

When you count, you normally use Base 10. (What this means is that each digit is valued as 10 times as much as the one to the right of it.) For example:

1
10 = 1 x 10
100 = 10 x 10
1,000 = 10 x 10 x 10
10,000 = 10 x 10 x 10 x 10
and so on.[1]

When we see a number like 423, we know that this is really:

(4 x 100) + (2 x 10) + 3

Digital electronics only have 2 states - HIGH and LOW (or ON and OFF). These are normally represented as 0 and 1. So in base 2 (commonly called binary), each digit is valued as 2 times as much as the one to the right of it. For example:

---

[1]Many people think we use base 10 because we have 10 fingers.

1
10 = 1 x 2
100 = 2 x 2 (4)
1000 = 2 x 2 x 2 (8)
1 0000 = 2 x 2 x 2 x 2 (16)
and so on.[2]

So when a computer sees 1101, we know that this is really:

(1 x 8) + (1 x 4) + (0 x 2) + (1 x 1) or 13 (in base 10)

It turns out that you can enter binary values in your code by starting them with a 0b.

```
int value = 0b1101;
```

Now, it turns out that this would be a lot of typing for numbers. Imagine 200:

(1 x 128) + (1 x 64) + (0 x 32) + (0 x 16) + (1 x 8) + (0 x 4) + (0x 2) + (0x 1)

```
int value = 0b11001000;
```

Computer Programmers don't like extra work. (Otherwise they wouldn't program computers to do things for them.) Most computers work on the concept of bytes which are 8-bits (so 8 "digits" in base 2.) In order to make it easier to type in (but still easy to convert back and forth to binary), they use base 16 (commonly called hexadecimal). In base 16:

1
10 = 1 x 16 (16)
100 = 16 x 16 (256)
1000 = 16 x 16 x 16 (4096)
and so on.

(You may have noticed that earlier I had a space after 4 digits in base 2. This is a convention because 4 digits in base 2 convert exactly to 1 digit in base 16.) There is one problem. We only have numbers 0-9 because we are used to base 10. Entirely new symbols could have been invented, but instead the solution is that we use letters. (A = 10, B = 11, C = 12, D = 13, E = 14, and F = 15)

So to represent 200 (base 10) in base 16, this is:

---

[2]Now you can appreciate the programmer's joke: There are 10 kinds of people in the world, those that understand binary and those that don't.

C8

(12 * 16) + (8 * 1)

192+8

200

We can put this in our code by starting with 0x to let the compiler know we are entering hexadecimal. (This is one of the few occurrences where you can use either lower or upper case letters and it doesn't make a difference.)

```
int value = 0xC8;
```

Note that there is absolutely no difference to the computer whether you say:

```
int value = 200;
int value = 0b11001000;
int value = 0xC8;
```

## 6.2 Using graphics

Ok, our detour is over. Now let's actually put some graphics on our LCD. This display has pixels (small dots) that can be either on or off. The controller chip represents on as a "1" and off as a "0". (Sound like binary?)

We write a column of 8 pixels to the display at one time. So, if we wanted all 8 to be on, we could send *0b11111111* (binary) or *0xFF* (hexadecimal). If we wanted all 8 to be off, we could send *0b00000000* or *0x00*[3] To give an example, what if we wanted to send a picture that was a diagonal line, like the following:

Since we send data to the LCD one *column* at a time, this would be: *0b00000001, 0b00000010, 0b00000100, 0b00001000, 0b00010000, 0b00100000, 0b01000000, 0b10000000*. (Or since programmers typically use base 16 in

---

[3]Yes, you could type in 0b0 or 0x0. I am trying to show the value of all 8 pixels here.

their programs instead of base 2, it would look like: *0x01, 0x02, 0x04, 0x08, 0x10, 0x20, 0x40, 0x80*). Notice the order. The top pixel in each column is represented as 1, next is 2, next is 4, and so on.

You could use this method and some graph paper and figure out exactly what to send. This would be difficult and would take a while (and would be easy to make a mistake.)

Luckily, there is an easier and better way.

A friend of mine (Jordan Liggitt) graciously wrote a program that will run on any modern browser and generate the code you need in your program. Bring up your web browser, and either open the file 8544.html on your USB key or http://www.introtoarduino.com/utils/pcd8544.html

Here is what it will look like when you first bring it up:

You can change the image width to any number up to the width of the display. But the image height can only be done in sets of 8. To turn a pixel "on" (dark) just click on the square. You can right-click to turn a pixel back "off". Here we use it to make a graphic that looks like a thermometer to put on the display:

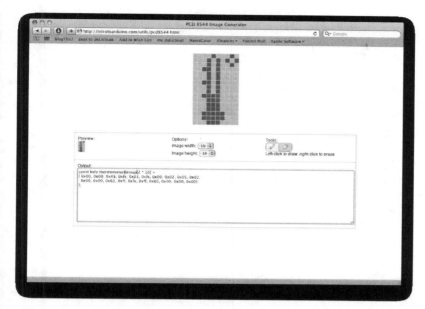

After you have drawn it, you can select the text in the output box and copy it (using Ctrl-C on a PC or Cmd-C on a mac) and then paste it into your Arduino program (using Ctrl-V on a PC or Cmd-V on a mac.) - If you make a mistake you can also copy it out of your program and paste it into the "output" box and the program will let you start there. If you have any problems, reload the web page and try again.

Let's use the same circuit and program from section 5.5and just add some graphics to pretty it up.

The entire program is shown first, and then we will go through the new portions.

Listing 6.1: temp_lcd_graphic/temp_lcd_graphic.pde

```
1  #include <PCD8544.h>
2
3  const int kPin_CLK = 5;
4  const int kPin_DIN = 6;
5  const int kPin_DC = 7;
6  const int kPin_RESET = 8;
```

```
7   const int kPin_Temp = A0;
8
9   PCD8544 lcd(kPin_CLK, kPin_DIN, kPin_DC, kPin_RESET);
10
11  // A bitmap graphic (5x1) of a degree symbol
12  const int DEGREE_WIDTH = 5;
13  const int DEGREE_HEIGHT = 1;
14  const byte degreesBitmap[1 * 5] = {
15    0x00, 0x07, 0x05, 0x07, 0x00 };
16
17  // A bitmap graphic (10x2) of a thermometer...
18  const int THERMO_WIDTH = 10;
19  const int THERMO_HEIGHT = 2;
20  const byte thermometerBitmap[2 * 10] =
21  {
22    0x00, 0x00, 0x48, 0xfe, 0x01, 0xfe, 0x00, 0x02, 0x05, 0x02,
23    0x00, 0x00, 0x62, 0xff, 0xfe, 0xff, 0x60, 0x00, 0x00, 0x00↩
          ↪ };
24
25  const int LCD_WIDTH = 84;
26  const int LCD_HEIGHT = 6;
27
28  void setup()
29  {
30    lcd.init();
31    lcd.setCursor(10,0);
32    lcd.print("Temperature:");
33    lcd.setCursor((LCD_WIDTH-THERMO_WIDTH) / 2, 3);
34    lcd.drawBitmap(thermometerBitmap, THERMO_WIDTH, ↩
          ↪ THERMO_HEIGHT);
35  }
36
37  void loop()
38  {
39    float temperatureC = getTemperatureC();
40    // now convert to Fahrenheit
41    float temperatureF = convertToF(temperatureC);
42
43    lcd.setCursor(21,1);
```

```
44    lcd.print(temperatureF);
45    lcd.drawBitmap(degreesBitmap, DEGREE_WIDTH, DEGREE_HEIGHT);
46    lcd.print(" F");
47    lcd.setCursor(21, 2);
48    lcd.print(temperatureC);
49    lcd.drawBitmap(degreesBitmap, DEGREE_WIDTH, DEGREE_HEIGHT);
50    lcd.print(" C");
51
52    delay(500);
53  }
54
55  float getTemperatureC()
56  {
57    int reading = analogRead(kPin_Temp);
58
59    float voltage = (reading * 5.0) / 1024;
60    // convert from 10 mv per degree with 500mV offset
61    // to degrees ((voltage - 500mV) * 100)
62    return (voltage - 0.5) * 100;
63  }
64
65  float convertToF(float temperatureC)
66  {
67    return (temperatureC * 9.0 / 5.0) + 32.0;
68  }
```

Most of this code is the same as in section 5.5. But let's go through the new portions.

```
11  // A bitmap graphic (5x1) of a degree symbol
12  const int DEGREE_WIDTH = 5;
13  const int DEGREE_HEIGHT = 1;
14  const byte degreesBitmap[1 * 5] = {
```

This defines a small graphic (5 pixels wide by 1 "line" (8 pixels) high) that we are going to use as a degree symbol.

```
17  // A bitmap graphic (10x2) of a thermometer...
18  const int THERMO_WIDTH = 10;
19  const int THERMO_HEIGHT = 2;
```

```
20  const byte thermometerBitmap[2 * 10] =
21  {
22    0x00, 0x00, 0x48, 0xfe, 0x01, 0xfe, 0x00, 0x02, 0x05, 0x02,
23    0x00, 0x00, 0x62, 0xff, 0xfe, 0xff, 0x60, 0x00, 0x00, 0x00↩
         ↪ };
```

This defines a graphic of a thermometer. (10 pixels wide by 2 "lines" (remember each line is 8 pixels, so it is 16 pixels high))

```
25  const int LCD_WIDTH = 84;
26  const int LCD_HEIGHT = 6;
```

Here we define the width and height of the LCD. We are going to use this later to calculate where to place something so it is centered.

```
33    lcd.setCursor((LCD_WIDTH-THERMO_WIDTH) / 2, 3);
34    lcd.drawBitmap(thermometerBitmap, THERMO_WIDTH, ↩
         ↪ THERMO_HEIGHT);
```

Here we use a neat trick to figure out where something should be centered. To center a graphic, you can simply start it at $\frac{lcdWidth-graphicWidth}{2}$. You may have to do a couple of examples to convince yourself that it works, but it always does. We use this to figure out the starting column. We start the starting "line" at 3 so it is below our display. (remember that the lines are 0 based, so this is actually at the fourth line.) We then call *drawBitmap()* to draw the bitmap. (A bitmap is the name of a graphic where you are giving the exact pixels that should be on or off.)

```
45    lcd.drawBitmap(degreesBitmap, DEGREE_WIDTH, DEGREE_HEIGHT);
```

This simply draws the small degree bitmap. (This happens again in line 49 but we aren't showing it because it is exactly the same.)

## 6.3 Making a Chart

Now, we are going to make a program that not only shows the temperature but shows a graph of the recent measurements (so you can tell if it is getting warmer or cooler.) Again, we will show the entire program first and then we will go through the new portions afterwards. (We are going to remove the Celsius temperature to have room for the graph.)

Listing 6.2: temp_lcd_graphic_chart/temp_lcd_graphic_chart.pde

```
#include <PCD8544.h>

const int kPin_CLK = 5;
const int kPin_DIN = 6;
const int kPin_DC = 7;
const int kPin_RESET = 8;
const int kPin_Temp = A0;

PCD8544 lcd(kPin_CLK, kPin_DIN, kPin_DC, kPin_RESET);

// A bitmap graphic (5x1) of a degree symbol
const int DEGREE_WIDTH = 5;
const int DEGREE_HEIGHT = 1;
const byte degreesBitmap[] = { 0x00, 0x07, 0x05, 0x07, 0x00 ↩
    ↪ };

// A bitmap graphic (10x2) of a thermometer...
const int THERMO_WIDTH = 10;
const int THERMO_HEIGHT = 2;
const byte thermometerBitmap[] =
{ 0x00, 0x00, 0x48, 0xfe, 0x01, 0xfe, 0x00, 0x02, 0x05, 0x02,
  0x00, 0x00, 0x62, 0xff, 0xfe, 0xff, 0x60, 0x00, 0x00, 0x00↩
    ↪ };

const int LCD_WIDTH = 84;
const int LCD_HEIGHT = 6;
const int GRAPH_HEIGHT = 5;

const int MIN_TEMP = 50;
const int MAX_TEMP = 100;

void setup()
{
  lcd.init();
```

81

```
33    lcd.setCursor(10,0);
34    lcd.print("Temperature:");
35    lcd.setCursor(0, LCD_HEIGHT - THERMO_HEIGHT);
36    lcd.drawBitmap(thermometerBitmap, THERMO_WIDTH, ←
          ↪ THERMO_HEIGHT);
37  }
38
39  int xChart = LCD_WIDTH;
40
41  void loop()
42  {
43    float temperatureC = getTemperatureC();
44     // now convert to Fahrenheit
45    float temperatureF = convertToF(temperatureC);
46
47    lcd.setCursor(21,1);
48    lcd.print(temperatureF);
49    lcd.drawBitmap(degreesBitmap, DEGREE_WIDTH, DEGREE_HEIGHT);
50    lcd.print(" F");
51    if(xChart >= LCD_WIDTH){
52      xChart = THERMO_WIDTH + 2;
53    }
54    lcd.setCursor(xChart, 2);
55    int dataHeight = map(temperatureF, MIN_TEMP, MAX_TEMP, 0, ←
          ↪ GRAPH_HEIGHT * 8);
56
57    drawColumn(dataHeight);
58    drawColumn(0);   // marker to see current chart position
59    xChart++;
60
61    delay(500);
62  }
63
64  float getTemperatureC()
65  {
66    int reading = analogRead(kPin_Temp);
67
68    float voltage = (reading * 5.0) / 1024;
69    // convert from 10 mv per degree with 500mV offset
```

```
70     // to degrees ((voltage - 500mV) * 100)
71     return (voltage - 0.5) * 100;
72  }
73
74  float convertToF(float temperatureC)
75  {
76      return (temperatureC * 9.0 / 5.0) + 32.0;
77  }
78
79  const byte dataBitmap[] =
80  {0x00, 0x80, 0xC0, 0xE0, 0xF0, 0xF8, 0xFC, 0xFE};
81
82  void drawColumn(unsigned int value)
83  {
84      byte graphBitmap[GRAPH_HEIGHT];
85      int i;
86
87      if(value > (GRAPH_HEIGHT * 8)){
88        value = GRAPH_HEIGHT * 8;
89      }
90      // value is number of pixels to draw
91
92      //1. clear all pixels in graphBitmap
93      for(i = 0; i < GRAPH_HEIGHT; i++){
94        graphBitmap[i] = 0x00;
95      }
96
97      //2. Fill all of the ones that should be completely full
98      i = 0;
99      while(value >= 8){
100         graphBitmap[GRAPH_HEIGHT - 1 - i] = 0xFF;
101         value -= 8;
102         i++;
103     }
104     if(i != GRAPH_HEIGHT){
105         graphBitmap[GRAPH_HEIGHT - 1 - i] = dataBitmap[value];
106     }
107     lcd.drawBitmap(graphBitmap, 1, GRAPH_HEIGHT);
108 }
```

Most of this code is the same as in section6.2, so we'll focus only on the differences.

```
25  const int GRAPH_HEIGHT = 5;
```

Here we define the height of the graph in "lines". (5 lines at 8 pixels per line, means that our graph will be 40 pixels high.

```
25  const int MIN_TEMP = 50;
26  const int MAX_TEMP = 100;
```

This just defines what the bottom and top values for our graph will be. There is no science here, I just picked two values that would likely cover anything we would have as a room temperature.

```
35  lcd.setCursor(0, LCD_HEIGHT - THERMO_HEIGHT);
36  lcd.drawBitmap(thermometerBitmap, THERMO_WIDTH, ↩
        ↪ THERMO_HEIGHT);
```

To figure out where to put the thermometer graphic, we are subtracting the height of the thermometer graphic from the height of the LCD. This will put the thermometer graphic in the lower left corner.

```
39  int xChart = LCD_WIDTH;
```

We are making a new variable to keep track of where we are on our chart. The initial value will be LCD_WIDTH. (This is a global variable so it could have been above *setup()*. I put it here so it will be close to the *loop()* function.)

```
51  if(xChart >= LCD_WIDTH){
52    xChart = THERMO_WIDTH + 2;
53  }
54  lcd.setCursor(xChart, 2);
```

If our *xChart* is at the edge of the screen (or past it), then we reset it to be 2 after the thermometer width. The 2 is just to give some "space" after the graphic before the chart. (You may notice that since the initial value was *LCD_WIDTH*, the first time through it will be reset like this. This is done so if we decide to change the spacing, it only has to be done one place. We then set the cursor so that the next thing we send to the LCD will be at this location.

```
55    int dataHeight = map(temperatureF, MIN_TEMP, MAX_TEMP, 0, ←
         ↪ GRAPH_HEIGHT * 8);
56
57    drawColumn(dataHeight);
58    drawColumn(0);   // marker to see current chart position
59    xChart++;
```

We calculate the height of the current column in the graph by using our old friend the *map()* function (from section 3.2.2). Then we call *drawColumn()* to draw the column. We then call *drawColumn()* with zero so it will draw an empty column after the one that was just drawn. This gives a visual indicator of where we are. Lastly we increment *xChart* so that we will be at the next spot in the graph next time we come here.

Most of the new stuff is in our *drawColumn()* function. This takes a value which is the "height" of the line to draw. The idea of the function is to quickly add "full" segments of 8 and then calculate the size of the last segment.

```
87    if(value > (GRAPH_HEIGHT * 8)){
88       value = GRAPH_HEIGHT * 8;
89    }
90    // value is number of pixels to draw
```

The first thing we do is make sure our value is not larger than it should be. This *should* never occur, but if it does we will write past the end of our array which is really bad and difficult to debug so it is worth it to check.

```
92    //1. clear all pixels in graphBitmap
93    for(i = 0; i < GRAPH_HEIGHT; i++){
94       graphBitmap[i] = 0x00;
95    }
```

Then we set the value of everything in *graphBitmap* to zero. (all pixels off). We do this so that we don't have to worry about what started in this array. (since it wasn't given a default value.)

```
98    i = 0;
```

85

```
 99    while(value >= 8){
100        graphBitmap[GRAPH_HEIGHT - 1 - i] = 0xFF;
101        value -= 8;
102        i++;
103    }
104    if(i != GRAPH_HEIGHT){
105        graphBitmap[GRAPH_HEIGHT - 1 - i] = dataBitmap[value];
106    }
```

This piece is tricky and you will probably need to run several examples through it to convince yourself that it works.

Let's do one together and then you can do as many as it takes for you to understand it. How about if value == 20.

```
99:   is value >= 8 - Yes, 20 is greater than 8.
100:  graphBitmap[GRAPH_HEIGHT - 1 - i] = 0xFF // all turned on
```
since GRAPH_HEIGHT is 5 and i is 0, then this will set graphBitmap[4] to 0xFF
```
101:  value -= 8.  Now value = 12.
102:  i++.  (i is now 1)
99:   is value >= 8.  Yes, 12 is greater than 8.
100:  graphBitmap[GRAPH_HEIGHT - 1 - i (1)] = 0xFF
```
since GRAPH_HEIGHT is 5 and i is 1, then this will set graphBitmap[3] to 0xFF
```
101:  value -= 8.  Now value = 4.
102:  i++ (i is now 2)
99:   is value >=8.  No, 4 is not greater than 8
104:  if(i != GRAPH_HEIGHT) (it isn't, i = 2, GRAPH_HEIGHT = 5)
105:  graphBitmap[GRAPH_HEIGHT - 1 - i (2)] = dataBitmap[value (4)]
```
since GRAPH_HEIGHT is 5 and i is 2, then this will set graphBitmap[2] to the value of dataBitmap[4] which is 0xF0.

So at the end, our *graphBitmap* will look like :

*0x00, 0x00, 0xF0, 0xFF, 0xFF*

(or in binary: *0b00000000, 0b00000000, 0b11110000, 0b11111111, 0b11111111*)

## 6.4 Exercises

1. Change the circuit and the program to have a button connected, and when the button is pressed the graph starts over.

2. Change the circuit and the program so there is a button that lets you change between Celsius and Farenheit.

3. SUPER CHALLENGE: Change the program to change the scale of the graph to have an auto-scale. (ie, At any time the graph has at the bottom the minimum temp observed, and the top is the maximum temp observed. Remove the thermometer graphic and show the scale of the graph on the LCD.)

# Chapter 7

# Sensors Galore

## 7.1 Introduction

The purpose of this chapter is to give you a taste of the wide variety of different types of sensors that you can hook up to a micro-controller. For this chapter, we will have four inexpensive sensors. They will detect light, tilt, magnetic field, and vibrations.

## 7.2 Photo Cell (Light Sensor)

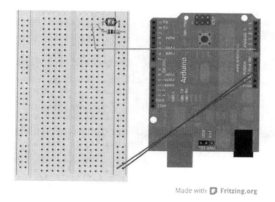

Made with **Fritzing.org**

1. Connect the far right column to GND on the Arduino.

2. Connect the next to right column to +5V on the Arduino.

3. Connect a 10kΩ (brown, black, orange) resistor on the far right and i2.

4. Connect one end of the photo cell in the next to right and the other end in j2.

5. Connect h2 to A0 on the Arduino.

The photo cell we are using acts like a potentiometer that has lower resistance the more light it sees. This is not a high precision instrument that measures exactly how much light there is. But it can be used to know whether a light is on in a room. You could also put it inside a drawer and know when it is opened.

Here is some sample code:

Listing 7.1: photocell/photocell.pde

```
1  const int kPin_Photocell = A0;
2
3  void setup()
4  {
5    Serial.begin(9600);
6  }
7
8  void loop()
9  {
10   int value = analogRead(kPin_Photocell);
11
12   Serial.print("Analog Reading = ");
13   Serial.print(value);
14   if(value < 200){
15     Serial.println(" - Dark");
16   }else if(value < 400){
17     Serial.println(" - Dim");
18   }
19   else if(value < 600){
20     Serial.println(" - Light");
21   }
22   else if(value < 800){
23     Serial.println(" - Bright");
```

```
24      }
25      else{
26         Serial.println(" - Very Bright");
27      }
28      delay(1000);
29   }
```

The numbers we are comparing to in this program were determined by experimenting. They could be different for your photo sensor and resistor. Change the comparisons until the words reflect what you think should be accurate. The important thing to know is that higher values mean more light.

## 7.3 Tilt Sensor

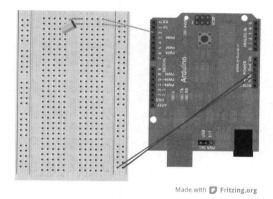

Made with **[]** Fritzing.org

1. Connect the far right column to GND on the Arduino.

2. Connect the next to right column to +5V on the Arduino.

3. Put the Tilt sensor in f1 and f2.

4. Connect j1 to 2 on the Arduino.

5. Connect j2 to the far right column (GND).

A tilt sensor is a switch that can determine when it is tilted. It works by having a metal ball inside and when it is tilted the ball is over the two contacts, so electricity can flow through the ball.

(This code uses the LED next to "L". If you want to hook up an LED and connect it to pin 13, you can.)

Listing 7.2: tiltsensor/tiltsensor.pde

```
1   const int kPin_Tilt = 3;
2   const int kPin_LED  = 13;
3
4   void setup()
5   {
6     pinMode(kPin_Tilt, INPUT);
7     digitalWrite(kPin_Tilt, HIGH);   // turn on built-in pull-up↩
          ↪  resistor
8     pinMode(kPin_LED, OUTPUT);
9   }
10
11  void loop()
12  {
13    if(digitalRead(kPin_Tilt) == HIGH){
14      digitalWrite(kPin_LED, LOW);
15    }
16    else{
17      digitalWrite(kPin_LED, HIGH);
18    }
19  }
```

You'll notice that we use the pull-up resistor just like we did with the push-buttons in section 3.1, so *LOW* means that it isn't tilted. and *HIGH* means that it is.

## 7.4 Reed Switch (Magnetic Field Detector)

Made with **Fritzing.org**

1. Connect the far right column to GND on the Arduino

2. Connect the next to right column to +5V on the Arduino

3. Connect the reed switch in the far right column (GND) and h7 (If your reed switch is bigger, f7 will work as well.)

4. Connect g7 and pin 2 on the Arduino.

A Reed switch is just like the pushbutton switch we did in Section 3.1. However, instead of pushing a button, a reed switch is closed when a magnet is near it. This can be used when you can't have things physically touch. A good example of a reed switch is to know when a door or window is open or closed.

Here is some sample code:

(This code uses the LED next to "L". If you want to hook up an LED and connect it to pin 13, you can.)

Listing 7.3: reed1/reed1.pde

```
1  const int kPinReedSwitch = 2;
2  const int kPinLed = 13;
3
4  void setup()
5  {
```

```
6    pinMode(kPinReedSwitch, INPUT);
7    digitalWrite(kPinReedSwitch, HIGH); // turn on pullup ↩
        ↪ resistor
8    pinMode(kPinLed, OUTPUT);
9  }
10
11 void loop()
12 {
13   if(digitalRead(kPinReedSwitch) == LOW){
14     digitalWrite(kPinLed, HIGH);
15   }
16   else{
17     digitalWrite(kPinLed, LOW);
18   }
19 }
```

## 7.5 Piezo Element (Vibration sensor)

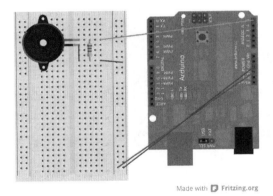

Made with **D** Fritzing.org

1. Connect the far right column to GND on the Arduino.

2. Connect the next to right column to +5V on the Arduino.

3. Plug the piezo in f5 and f9.

4. Put a 1MΩ (brown, brown, green) resistor in h5 and h9.

5. Connect j9 to far right column (GND).

6. Connect j5 to A5 on Arduino.

This sensor is a piezo element. It can be used as either a speaker or to detect vibrations like knocking. Here we are using it to detect knocking. Whenever we spot a transition, we delay for 20ms to make sure it is a knock and not left over vibrations from an earlier knock. You can experiment with this value.

(This code uses the LED next to "L". If you want to hook up an LED and connect it to pin 13, you can.)

Listing 7.4: knock1/knock1.pde

```
1  const int kPinSensor = A5;
2  const int kPinLed = 13;
3  const int k_threshold = 100;
4
5  int ledState = LOW;          // variable used to store the ←
       ↪ last LED status, to toggle the light
6
7  void setup()
8  {
9    pinMode(kPinLed, OUTPUT); // declare the ledPin as as ←
         ↪ OUTPUT
10 }
11
12 void loop()
13 {
14   int val = analogRead(kPinSensor);
15
16   if (val >= k_threshold) {
17     ledState = !ledState;    // toggle the value of ledState
18     digitalWrite(kPinLed, ledState);
19     delay(20);  // for debouncing
20   }
21 }
```

The threshold is just to make sure it was a real knock, and not some other vibration from the room. You can adjust this value to see what works best for you. A5 was just selected on the Arduino because I was originally using this in part of a larger project. You can use any of the analog inputs (as long as your circuit and program match)

## 7.6 Exercises

1. Hook up a photo cell and an LED. Have the LED shine brighter (using PWM) when there is more light and dimmer when there is less light.

2. Hook up a Tilt Sensor and the speaker. Have activating of the tilt sensor make an alarm go off.

3. Use the reed switch and the magnet to make a sound when the magnet is close.

4. Hook up the piezo element and use it to play a tune after someone knocks.

   a) HUGE CHALLENGE: Light an LED after someone knocks a correct pattern (say 3 in a row followed by silence.)

# Chapter 8

# Making a rubber band gun

## 8.1 One Servo

A servo is a motor that you can command to go to a particular angle. A servo has 3 pins. Power (normally red), Ground (normally black), and a signal pin (normally white.); Servos are given a command of what angle to turn to (between 0 and 180) and they turn to precisely that location. This makes them a favorite for a lot of uses because they are relatively easy to control.

The Arduino language has support for servos built-in which makes the servos really easy to use. To start with we'll hook up one servo and a potentiometer.

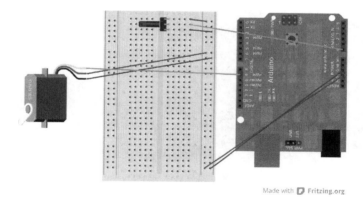

Made with **Fritzing.org**

1. Connect the far right column to GND on the Arduino.

2. Connect the next to right column to +5V on the Arduino.

3. Put the potentiometer in f1, f2, f3.

4. Connect j1 to the next to right column (+5V).

5. Connect j3 to the far right column (GND).

6. Connect j2 to A0 on the Arduino.

7. Connect the red wire of the servo to +5V (next to right column).

8. Connect the black wire of the servo to GND (far right column).

9. Connect the white wire of the servo to pin 9 on the Arduino.

This program lets you turn the potentiometer and the servo rotates as you turn it.

Listing 8.1: servo1/servo1.pde

```
1  #include <Servo.h>
2
3  Servo servo1;
4
5  const int kPinPot = A0;
6  const int kPinServo1 = 9;
7
8  void setup()
9  {
10    servo1.attach(kPinServo1);
11  }
12
13  void loop()
14  {
15    int val = analogRead(kPinPot);
16    val = map(val, 0, 1023, 0, 180);
17    servo1.write(val);
18    delay(15);
19  }
```

There are only two things in here that are new. One is attaching the servo (telling it what pin it is on.) The second is sending it a value (0 to 180) for the angle.

## 8.2 Joystick

We have a thumb joystick that we will use. It is made up of 2 potentiometers (one for the x-axis and one for the y-axis) and a switch (for when the button is pressed).

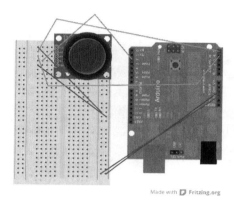

Made with **D** Fritzing.org

1. Connect the far right column to GND on the Arduino.

2. Connect the next to right column to +5V on the Arduino.

3. Put the Joystick breakout board in d1-d5.

4. Connect a1 to the next to right column (+5V).

5. Connect a2 to A5 on the Arduino..

6. Connect a3 to A4 on the Arduino.

7. Connect a4 to pin 2 on the Arduino.

8. Connect a5 to the far right column (GND).

We allow for a "dead zone" in the middle of the joystick where we don't register as any direction. This helps us not to have to worry about the "jitter" that is inherent in mechanical devices. You can see the values change in the serial monitor.

Listing 8.2: joystick/joystick.pde

```
1   const int kPinJoystickX = A5;
2   const int kPinJoystickY = A4;
3   const int kPinJoystickFire = 2;
4
5   const int JOYX_LEFT = 300;
6   const int JOYX_RIGHT = 700;
7   const int JOYY_UP = 700;
8   const int JOYY_DOWN = 300;
9
10  void setup()
11  {
12    pinMode(kPinJoystickFire, INPUT);
13    digitalWrite(kPinJoystickFire, HIGH);   // turn on pull-up ←
          ↪ resistor
14    Serial.begin(9600);
15  }
16
17  void loop()
18  {
19    int xVal = analogRead(kPinJoystickX);
20    int yVal = analogRead(kPinJoystickY);
21
22    Serial.print("x = ");
23    Serial.print(xVal);
24    Serial.print(" y = ");
25    Serial.print(yVal);
26    Serial.print(' ');
27
28    if(xVal < JOYX_LEFT){
29      Serial.print('L');
30    }
31    else if(xVal > JOYX_RIGHT){
32      Serial.print('R');
33    }
34    if(yVal < JOYY_DOWN){
35      Serial.print('D');
36    }
```

```
37    else if(yVal > JOYY_UP){
38        Serial.print('U');
39    }
40    if(digitalRead(kPinJoystickFire) == LOW){
41        Serial.print("+F");
42    }
43    Serial.println();
44
45    delay(100);   // Keep from overwhelming serial
46 }
```

Since the readings from the joystick are within a range of 0 to 1023, we break the range down into sections. We call less than 300 LEFT (or UP), greater than 700 RIGHT (or DOWN), and just let everything in the middle count as CENTER.

The +F is to show that the joystick has been pressed down.

## 8.3 Pan/Tilt bracket

We have attached two servos to the pan/tilt bracket. That will allow us to pan (0-180 degrees) and tilt (0-180 degrees). Let's combine that with the joystick for aiming.

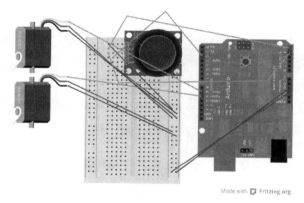

Made with 🗲 Fritzing.org

(HINT: If you don't take apart the circuit in the last section, you can start with step 9.)

1. Connect the far right column to GND on the Arduino.

2. Connect the next to right column to +5V on the Arduino.

3. Put the Joystick breakout board in d1-d5.

4. Connect a1 on breadboard to the next to right column (+5V).

5. Connect a2 on breadboard to A5 on the Arduino.

6. Connect a3 on breadboard to A4 on the Arduino.

7. Connect a4 on breadboard to pin 2 on the Arduino.

8. Connect a5 on breadboard to the far right column (GND).

9. Connect the black wire of the servo on bottom (the pan servo) to the far right column (GND)

10. Connect the red wire of the servo on bottom (the pan servo) to the next to right column (+5V)

11. Connect the white wire of the servo on bottom (the pan servo) to pin 9 on the Arduino.

12. Connect the black wire of the servo in the middle (the tilt servo) to the far right column (GND)

13. Connect the red wire of the servo in the middle (the tilt servo) to the next to right column (+5V)

14. Connect the white wire of the servo in the middle (the tilt servo) to pin 10 on the Arduino.

Listing 8.3: pantilt/pantilt.pde

```
1   #include <Servo.h>
2
3   const int kPinJoystickX = A5;
4   const int kPinJoystickY = A4;
```

```
5   const int kPinJoystickFire = 2;
6   const int kPinServoPan = 9;
7   const int kPinServoTilt = 10;
8
9   const int JOYX_LEFT = 300;
10  const int JOYX_RIGHT = 700;
11  const int JOYY_UP = 700;
12  const int JOYY_DOWN = 300;
13
14  Servo panServo;
15  Servo tiltServo;
16
17  int panAngle = 0;
18  int tiltAngle = 90;
19
20  void setup()
21  {
22    panServo.attach(kPinServoPan);
23    tiltServo.attach(kPinServoTilt);
24  }
25
26  void loop()
27  {
28    int xVal = analogRead(kPinJoystickX);
29    int yVal = analogRead(kPinJoystickY);
30
31    if(xVal < JOYX_LEFT){
32      panAngle--;
33    }
34    else if(xVal > JOYX_RIGHT){
35      panAngle++;
36    }
37    if(yVal < JOYY_DOWN){
38      tiltAngle--;
39    }
40    else if(yVal > JOYY_UP){
41      tiltAngle++;
42    }
43    tiltAngle = constrain(tiltAngle, 0, 180);
```

```
44    panAngle = constrain(panAngle, 0, 180);

45

46    panServo.write(panAngle);
47    tiltServo.write(tiltAngle);
48    delay(20);   // wait for the servos to get there
49  }
```

Our old friend the `constrain()` function makes sure that we keep the panAngle and the tiltAngle within the values that the servos can do.

## 8.4 Adding a firing mechanism

If you aren't taking the class, you can download instructions and templates for how to make or buy the various components needed at `http://www.introtoarduino.com`

Now, we connect one more servo to actually fire the rubber band.

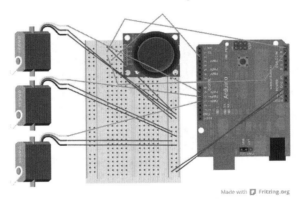

Made with 🗌 Fritzing.org

(HINT: If you don't take apart the circuit in the last section, you can start with step 15)

1. Connect the far right column to GND on the Arduino.

2. Connect the next to right column to +5V on the Arduino.

3. Put the Joystick breakout board in d1-d5.

4. Connect a1 on breadboard to the next to right column (+5V).

5. Connect a2 on breadboard to A5 on the Arduino.

6. Connect a3 on breadboard to A4 on the Arduino.

7. Connect a4 on breadboard to pin 2 on the Arduino.

8. Connect a5 on breadboard to the far right column (GND).

9. Connect the black wire of the servo on bottom (the pan servo) to the far right column (GND).

10. Connect the red wire of the servo on bottom (the pan servo) to the next to right column (+5V).

11. Connect the white wire of the servo on bottom (the pan servo) to pin 9 on the Arduino.

12. Connect the black wire of the servo in the middle (the tilt servo) to the far right column (GND).

13. Connect the red wire of the servo in the middle (the tilt servo) to the next to right column (+5V).

14. Connect the white wire of the servo in the middle (the tilt servo) to pin 10 on the Arduino.

15. Connect the black wire of the servo on the top (the fire servo) to the far right column (GND).

16. Connect the red wire of the servo on the top (the fire servo) to the next to right column (+5V).

17. Connect the white wire of the servo on the top (the fire servo) to pin 11 on the Arduino.

Listing 8.4: rubberBandGun/rubberBandGun.pde

```
1   #include <Servo.h>
2
3   const int kPinJoystickX = A5;
4   const int kPinJoystickY = A4;
5   const int kPinJoystickFire = 2;
6   const int kPinServoPan = 9;
7   const int kPinServoTilt = 10;
8   const int kPinServoFire = 11;
9
10  const int JOYX_LEFT = 300;
11  const int JOYX_RIGHT = 700;
12  const int JOYY_UP = 700;
13  const int JOYY_DOWN = 300;
14
15  Servo panServo;
16  Servo tiltServo;
17  Servo fireServo;
18
19  int panAngle = 90;
20  int tiltAngle = 90;
21  int fireAngle = 0;
22
23  void setup()
24  {
25    pinMode(kPinJoystickFire, INPUT);
26    digitalWrite(kPinJoystickFire, HIGH); // turn on pull-up ←
          ↪ resistor
27    fireServo.attach(kPinServoFire);
28    fireServo.write(0);
29    delay(500);
30    fireServo.detach();
31    panServo.attach(kPinServoPan);
32    tiltServo.attach(kPinServoTilt);
33  }
34
35  void loop()
36  {
```

```
37  int xVal = analogRead(kPinJoystickX);
38  int yVal = analogRead(kPinJoystickY);
39
40  if(xVal < JOYX_LEFT){
41    panAngle--;
42  }
43  else if(xVal > JOYX_RIGHT){
44    panAngle++;
45  }
46  if(yVal < JOYY_DOWN){
47    tiltAngle--;
48  }
49  else if(yVal > JOYY_UP){
50    tiltAngle++;
51  }
52  tiltAngle = constrain(tiltAngle, 0, 180);
53  panAngle = constrain(panAngle, 0, 180);
54
55  panServo.write(panAngle);
56  tiltServo.write(tiltAngle);
57  delay(20);   // wait for the servos to get there
58
59  if(digitalRead(kPinJoystickFire) == LOW){
60    fireServo.attach(kPinServoFire);
61    fireServo.write(180);
62    delay(500);
63    fireServo.write(0);
64    delay(500);
65    fireServo.detach();
66    while(digitalRead(kPinJoystickFire) == LOW){
67      // wait for it not to be low anymore
68    }
69  }
70 }
```

The reason why we attach and detach the firing servo is that we don't move it very often and we don't want to send it commands continuously when we won't use it very often. This is for power reasons.

The *fireServo.write(180)* is the line that actually fires the rubber band. Then it goes back to 0 so we can load the next rubber band on it.

## 8.5 Exercises

1. Hook up the joystick and 5 LEDs. One that shows when the joystick is pressed up, one for down, one for left, one for right, and one for fire.

2. Make a servo do a slow sweep from 0 to 180 and then back again.

3. CHALLENGE: After firing a rubber band, play a victory tune!

# Chapter 9

# Make your own project!

Now it is time to unleash your creativity. Hopefully as we have gone through these sections, you have started to think of other things that would be neat to make. One of the great things about micro-controllers is how many things you can make.

It is now time for you to make your own project. Below is a sample list of projects that you can make with the parts that are in your kit. Make something off this list or something you have thought of. Just make something!!

- A stopwatch (uses the LCD, push buttons)

- A count down timer (uses the LCD, push buttons, speaker)

- An alarm clock (Challenging, as you have to do all of the programming to allow the setting of the time) - (uses the LCD, push buttons, speaker)

- An alarm when the temperature goes out of a set range

- Let someone knock using the knock sensor and have the controller play it back (as either sound or lights)

- Make a dial that shows the temperature (use a servo and the temperature sensor)

- Make a dial that shows the amount of light (use a servo and the light sensor)

- Change tone playing on speaker based off of amount of light, or temperature

*Chapter 9 Make your own project!*

- Alarm going off when reed switch opens (to let you know when someone has opened a door)

- Data logger - time and temp, light - either on serial or LCD. As a bonus, allow scrolling using either the joystick or pushbuttons

- Morse code - one button dots, one button dashes. Saving/recording

- Enter message using joystick onto LCD, and then playback on speaker with morse code when a button is pressed

- Traffic light simulation - include push buttons for car sensors

- A metronome (uses the speaker, LCD and pushbuttons (or a potentiometer))

- If you have great ideas, please give them to me and I'll add them to future versions of the book!!

# Chapter 10

# Next Steps

If you enjoyed this book, then there is lots more you can learn. I would recommend looking at a few websites for inspiration. (Make sure you have your parent's permission and be careful of anyone that asks for contact information online.)

- http://www.arduino.cc

- http://www.sparkfun.com

- http://www.adafruit.com

- http://www.makezine.com

I would also recommend the book *Arduino Cookbook* by Michael Margolis. Here are a few ideas of more complicated projects that I have seen made with an Arduino.

- A box that will only open when it is at a certain location in the world (It connects a GPS to the Arduino. Search on "Reverse Geo-cache" to see examples.)

- An alarm clock that rolls away from you when it goes off

- An alarm clock that you set by tilting back and forth

- A Thermostat

- A controller for a 3D printer

- Robots

- A module that goes in a model rocket and keeps track of the acceleration so it can be charted upon recovery

- A full weather station (wind speed, rain amounts, humidity, temperature, barometer, etc.)

- and much, much more!!

I hope you have enjoyed this introduction. What you can create is limited only by your creativity (and budget!) Areas for future study would be interfacing with more types of sensors, more sophisticated programming, more powerful micro-controllers, and much much more!

This is the end of this book, but only the beginning of your journey! Please let me know what you have made as I will be excited to see your creations! You can contact me at: `alan@introtoarduino.com`

# Appendix A

# Arduino Reference

I have included this reference only for completeness. It describes everything that is part of the Arduino language. However, there is no attempt given to define or explain in the appendix. If there is something you are interested in more details, I suggest looking online at the much more comprehensive reference that is online at `http://www.arduino.cc/en/Reference/HomePage`.

Also the Arduino language is simply a processing step[1] done before handing the resulting code off to a C++ compiler. You can use any C or C++ reference online to get more information.

In fact, if you look online you'll notice that I used the same structure to split things up as they do online. The online reference is really good with examples for each one.

There are three main parts: structure, values (variables and constants), and functions.

---

[1] It puts a `#include` before the beginning, scans the file for functions and puts the prototypes at the top of the file, and then includes a `main()` function at the bottom that calls `setup()` and `loop()`

## A.1 Structure

### A.1.1 Control Structures

| Name | Brief Description |
|---|---|
| `if` | Covered in section 2.2 |
| `if...else` | Covered in section 2.3 |
| `for` | Covered in section 2.7 |
| `switch case` | Not covered in this text. This is a way to select between several different values. |
| `while` | Covered in section 2.4 |
| `do...while` | Not covered in this text. This is like a while statement except the code block always executes once and then the condition is evaluated. |
| `break` | Not covered in this text. When this is encountered, the code goes to the outside of the current block. (curly braces.) |
| `continue` | Not covered in this text. When this is encoutered, the code goes to the end of the current block. (and in a for or while loop it is evaluated again.) |
| `return` | Covered in section 5.2 |
| `goto` | Not covered in this text. When this is encountered the code jumps to the label specified. |

### A.1.2 Further Syntax

| Name | Brief Description |
|---|---|
| `;` (semicolon) | used to end a statement |
| `{}` (curly braces) | defines a block of code (often used as a function or following an if, else, while, or for) |
| `//` (single line comment) | Covered in section 1.7 |
| `/* */` (multi-line comment) | Covered in section 1.7 |
| `#define` | Covered in section 4.3 |
| `#include` | Covered in section 5.4.2 |

## A.1.3 Arithmetic Operators

| Operator | Meaning |
|---|---|
| = | assignment operator |
| + | addition operator |
| − | subtraction operator |
| * | multiplication operator |
| / | division - be aware that if you are using integers only the whole part is kept. It is NOT rounded. For example: 5 / 2 == 2 |
| % | modulo - This gives the remainder. For example: 5 % 2 == 1 |

## A.1.4 Comparison Operators

| Operator | Meaning |
|---|---|
| == | is equal to |
| != | is not equal to |
| < | is less than |
| > | is greater than |
| <= | is less than or equal to |
| >= | is greater than or equal to |

## A.1.5 Boolean Operators

| Operator | Example | Meaning |
|---|---|---|
| && | (A < 10) && (B > 5) | logical AND (return TRUE if condition A AND condition B are true, otherwise return FALSE.) |
| \|\| | (A < 10) \|\| (B > 5) | logical OR (return TRUE if condition A OR condition B is true, otherwise return FALSE.) |
| ! | !(A < 10) | logical NOT (return TRUE if condition A is false, otherwise return TRUE) |

## A.1.6 Pointer Access Operators

Pointers are very powerful but can also be fraught with danger. The easiest way to understand pointers is to know that to the computer, all data has a memory address. (where it lives in memory) An explanation of pointers is outside the scope of this book, but I am including the operators here for completeness.

| Operator | Brief Description |
|:---:|---|
| * | dereference operator |
| & | reference operator |

## A.1.7 Bitwise Operators

We have not talked about bitwise operators in this book. These are included only for completeness.

| Operator | Brief Description |
|:---:|---|
| & | bitwise and |
| / | bitwise or |
| ^ | bitwise xor |
| ~ | bitwise not |
| << | shift left |
| >> | shift right |

## A.1.8 Compound Operators

| Operator | Meaning | Example |
|---|---|---|
| ++ | increment | $x++$ means the same as $x = x + 1$ |
| -- | decrement | $x--$ means the same as $x = x - 1$ |
| += | compound addition | $x += 2$ means the same as $x = x + 2$ |
| -= | compound subtraction | $x -= 2$ means the same as $x = x - 2$ |
| *= | compound multiplication | $x *= 2$ means the same as $x = x * 2$ |
| /= | compound division | $x /= 2$ means the same as $x = x / 2$ |
| %= | compound modulo | $x \%= 2$ means the same as $x = x \% 2$ |
| &= | compound and | $x \&= 2$ means the same as $x = x \& 2$ |
| \|= | compound or | $x \|= 2$ means the same as $x = x \| 2$ |
| ^= | compound xor | $x \hat{\ }= 2$ means the same as $x = x \hat{\ } 2$ |
| <<= | compound shift left | $x <<= 2$ means the same as $x = x << 2$ |
| >>= | compound shift right | $x >>= 2$ means the same as $x = x >> 2$ |

## A.2 Variables

### A.2.1 Constants

| Name | Brief Description |
|---|---|
| *HIGH/LOW* | used to set pin state. See section 1.6 |
| *INPUT/OUTPUT* | used with pinMode. See section 1.6 |
| *true/false* | false = 0, true = not false |
| integer constants | when you put an integer in your code, can be followed by L for long or U for unsigned |
| floating point constants | when you put floating point number in your code. (you can use an e or E for scientific notation) |

### A.2.2 Data Types

| Name | Brief Definition |
|---|---|
| *void* | used only in function declarations - means it returns nothing |
| *boolean* | holds either true or false |
| *char* | -127 to 127 |
| *unsigned char* | 0 to 255 |
| *byte* | same as unsigned char |
| *int* | -32,7678 to 32,767 |
| *unsigned int* | 0 to 65,555 |
| *word* | same as unsigned int |
| *long* | -2,147,483,648 to 2,147,483,647 |
| *unsigned long* | 0 to 4,294,967,295 |
| *float* | -3.4028235E+38 to 3.4028235E+38 |
| *double* | (same as float) |
| string | array of characters - defined as *char strName[5];* |
| *String* | a String Object |
| array | See section 2.9 |

118

### A.2.3 Conversion

| Name | Brief Description |
|---|---|
| *char()* | converts to the char type |
| *byte()* | converts to the byte type |
| *int()* | converts to the int type |
| *word()* | converts to the word type |
| *long()* | converts to the long type |
| *float()* | converts to the float type |

### A.2.4 Variable Scope & Qualifiers

| Name | Brief Description |
|---|---|
| variable scope | Described in section 2.2 |
| *static* | preserve the data between calls, visible only to that scope (file or function) |
| *volatile* | for when a variable can be changed by something external. Normally in arduino, this is for variables that are changed in an interrupt service routine (ISR) |
| *const* | means the variable cannot be changed |

### A.2.5 Utilities

*sizeof()* - returns the size of a variable in bytes

## A.3 Functions

### A.3.1 Digital I/O

| Name | Brief Description |
|---|---|
| *pinMode()* | sets the pin as INPUT or OUTPUT |
| *digitalWrite()* | writes a value out on a pin (if output), or enables the pullup resistor (if input) |
| *digitalRead()* | reads a value in from a pin |

## A.3.2 Analog I/O

| Name | Brief Description |
|---|---|
| analogReference() | configures the reference voltage used for analog input |
| analogRead() | reads an analog voltage and converts to an integer value between 0 and 1023 |
| analogWrite() | uses PWM to write a value out on a pin. See section 3.1.2 for details |

## A.3.3 Advanced I/O

| Name | Brief Description |
|---|---|
| tone() | See section 4.3 for details |
| noTone() | See section 4.3 for details |
| shiftOut() | uses a data pin and a clock pin to send out data one bit at a time |
| shiftIn() | uses a data pin and a clock pin to read in data one bit at a time |
| pulseIn() | Will measure the duration of a pulse on a pin |

## A.3.4 Time

| Name | Brief Description |
|---|---|
| millis() | Returns number of milliseconds Arduino has been up (overflows after approximately 50 days) |
| micros() | Returns number of microseconds Arduino has been running current program. (overflows after approximately 70 minutes) |
| delay() | Pauses the program for the amount of time (in milliseconds) specified as parameter. |
| delayMicroseconds() | Pauses the program for the amount of time (in microseconds) specified as parameter. |

## A.3.5 Math

| Name | Brief Description |
|---|---|
| min() | returns the minimum of two values |
| max() | returns the maximum of two values |
| abs() | returns the absolute value |
| constrain() | See section 3.2.2 for details |
| map() | See section 3.1.2.2 for details |
| pow() | calculates the value of a number raised to a power |
| sqrt() | calculates the value of the square root of a number |

## A.3.6 Trigonometry

| Name | Brief Description |
|---|---|
| sin() | Calculates the sine of an angle (in radians) |
| cos() | Calculates the cosine of an angle (in radians) |
| tan() | Calculates the tangent of an angle (in radians) |

## A.3.7 Random Numbers

| Name | Brief Description |
|---|---|
| randomSeed() | initialize the pseudo-random number generator |
| random() | generate a pseudo-random number |

## A.3.8 Bits and Bytes

| Name | Brief Description |
|---|---|
| lowByte() | lowest byte of a variable |
| highByte() | highest byte of a variable |
| bitRead() | Reads a bit of a variable |
| bitWrite() | Writes a bit of a variable |
| bitSet() | sets a bit of a variable to 1 |
| bitClear() | sets a bit of a variable to 0 |
| bit() | the value of the specified bit |

### A.3.9 External Interrupts

| Name | Brief Description |
|------|-------------------|
| attachInterrupt() | specify a function to call when an interrupt occurrs |
| detachInterrupt() | turn off a given interrupt |

### A.3.10 Interrupts

| Name | Brief Description |
|------|-------------------|
| interrupts() | re-enable interrupts |
| noInterrupts() | disable interrupts |

### A.3.11 Communication

Serial Class - used partially in section 5.1. Full list of functions are:

| Name | Brief Description |
|------|-------------------|
| Serial.begin() | set the data rate |
| Serial.end() | disables serial communication |
| Serial.available() | Gets number of bytes available for reading (already in the receive buffer which holds 128 bytes) |
| Serial.read() | read incoming serial data (and removes from buffer) |
| Serial.peek() | returns the next byte of serial data without removing from buffer |
| Serial.flush() | removes all data in receive buffer |
| Serial.print() | prints data to the serial port as human-readable ASCII text |
| Serial.println() | prints data to the serial port as human-readable ASCII text followed by a newline |
| Serial.write() | sends data byte to the serial port |

## A.4 PCD8544 (LCD Controller) Library

| Name | Brief Description |
|---|---|
| *init()* | This needs to be called first, before you do anything else with the LCD. You can use this to tell the library which pins are under Arduino control. |
| *clear()* | This clears the screen (and sets the cursor to the upper left hand corner). |
| *setBacklight()* | If you connected a pin from the Arduino to the backlight on the LCD then you can use this function to control the backlight. You can call the function with either *true* (for on) or *false* (for off). |
| *setBacklight_PWM()* | If you connected a pin that is capable of PWM from the Arduino to the backlight on the LCD then you can use this function to control the brightness of the backlight. You can call this function with a value from 0 (off) to 255 (fully on). |
| *setInverse()* | You can call this function with *true* (light on dark background) or *false* (dark on light background). |
| *setCursor()* | This sets the location (pixelrow, line number) that the next *print()*, *write()*, or *drawBitmap()* will take effect at. |
| *print()* | This will print out the contents of a variable at the current location. You can call this with an integer or a float or a string. (A string is text in between quotation makrs (like we did in section 5.4.2) |
| *write()* | This is included for completeness. You should call *print()* instead which uses this function to send each individual character to the LCD. |
| *drawBitmap()* | This takes the bitmap followed by the number of columns (1-84) and the number of lines (1-6) of data being passed to it. |

A few notes on init(). There are four different ways you can use it:

1. The way we have used it throughout this book.

```
lcd.init(kPIN_CLK, kPin_DIN, kPin_DC, kPin_RESET);
```

2. Also having backlight under program control.

```
lcd.init(kPIN_CLK, kPin_DIN, kPin_DC, kPin_RESET, backlight);
```

3. Having backlight and CS (chip select) under program control. The reason you would want CS under control, is it allows you to reuse the CLK, DIN, DC, and RESET pins for other things since the device only listens on those lines when CS is low.

```
lcd.init(kPIN_CLK, kPin_DIN, kPin_DC, kPin_RESET, backlight, kPin_CS);
```

4. Having CS (chip select) under program control, but not the backlight.

```
lcd.init(kPin_CLK, kPin_DIN, kPin_DC, kPin_RESET, -1, kPin_CS);
```

# Appendix B

# Parts in Kit

## B.1 First used in Chapter 1

- Arduino Uno

- Arduino + Breadboard holder

- Breadboard

- LEDs

- 330 Ohm 1/4 Watt resistors

- Jumper Wires

- USB Flash memory with all software

- USB Cable

- Parts box

- 9V battery case

- 9V battery

## B.2 First used in Chapter 2

- NONE

## B.3 First used in Chapter 3

- Push Buttons (2)
- 10k Pot with knob (3)
- RGB LED

## B.4 First used in Chapter 4

- Speaker

## B.5 First used in Chapter 5

- Temp sensor (TMP36)
- LCD (84x48 graphical)

## B.6 First used in Chapter 6

- NONE

## B.7 First used in Chapter 7

- Piezeo (knock) Sensor
- 1M Ohm resistor
- Reed switch
- magnet
- Photo cell sensor
- 10k Ohm resistor
- Tilt switch

## B.8 First used in Chapter 8

- Servos

- joystick on Breakout board

- Pan tilt bracket

- Rubber band firing mechanism

# Appendix C

# Sample Solutions to Selected Exercises

These are just one way to solve the exercises. It is not the only way or even the best way. Try to solve the exercises yourself first before looking here. This is just in case you are stuck.

## C.1 Chapter 1 Solutions

Listing C.1: solutions/Chap1_1/Chap1_1.pde

```
1  const int kPinLed = 13;
2
3  void setup()
4  {
5
6    pinMode(kPinLed, OUTPUT);
7  }
8
9  void loop()
10 {
11   digitalWrite(kPinLed, HIGH);
12   delay(500);
13   digitalWrite(kPinLed, LOW);
14   delay(1000);
15 }
```

Listing C.2: solutions/Chap1_2/Chap1_2.pde

```
1  const int kPinLed = 2;
```

```
2
3  void setup()
4  {
5    pinMode(kPinLed, OUTPUT);
6  }
7
8  void loop()
9  {
10    digitalWrite(kPinLed, HIGH);
11    delay(500);
12    digitalWrite(kPinLed, LOW);
13    delay(1000);
14  }
```

Listing C.3: solutions/Chap1_3/Chap1_3.pde

```
1   const int kPinLed1 = 2;
2   const int kPinLed2 = 3;
3   const int kPinLed3 = 4;
4   const int kPinLed4 = 5;
5   const int kPinLed5 = 6;
6   const int kPinLed6 = 7;
7   const int kPinLed7 = 8;
8   const int kPinLed8 = 9;
9
10  void setup()
11  {
12    pinMode(kPinLed1, OUTPUT);
13    pinMode(kPinLed2, OUTPUT);
14    pinMode(kPinLed3, OUTPUT);
15    pinMode(kPinLed4, OUTPUT);
16    pinMode(kPinLed5, OUTPUT);
17    pinMode(kPinLed6, OUTPUT);
18    pinMode(kPinLed7, OUTPUT);
19    pinMode(kPinLed8, OUTPUT);
20  }
21
22  void loop()
23  {
```

```
24    // turn on the LEDs
25    digitalWrite(kPinLed1, HIGH);
26    delay(500);
27    digitalWrite(kPinLed2, HIGH);
28    delay(500);
29    digitalWrite(kPinLed3, HIGH);
30    delay(500);
31    digitalWrite(kPinLed4, HIGH);
32    delay(500);
33    digitalWrite(kPinLed5, HIGH);
34    delay(500);
35    digitalWrite(kPinLed6, HIGH);
36    delay(500);
37    digitalWrite(kPinLed7, HIGH);
38    delay(500);
39    digitalWrite(kPinLed8, HIGH);
40    delay(500);
41    // Now turn them off
42    digitalWrite(kPinLed1, LOW);
43    delay(500);
44    digitalWrite(kPinLed2, LOW);
45    delay(500);
46    digitalWrite(kPinLed3, LOW);
47    delay(500);
48    digitalWrite(kPinLed4, LOW);
49    delay(500);
50    digitalWrite(kPinLed5, LOW);
51    delay(500);
52    digitalWrite(kPinLed6, LOW);
53    delay(500);
54    digitalWrite(kPinLed7, LOW);
55    delay(500);
56    digitalWrite(kPinLed8, LOW);
57    delay(1000);   // wait 1 second with them all off before ←
          ↪ starting again
58  }
```

## C.2 Chapter 2 Solutions

Listing C.4: solutions/Chap2_1/Chap2_1.pde

```
1   const int kPinLed = 9;
2
3   void setup()
4   {
5     pinMode(kPinLed, OUTPUT);
6   }
7
8   void loop()
9   {
10    for(int i = 0; i < 4; i++){
11      digitalWrite(kPinLed, HIGH);
12      delay(200);
13      digitalWrite(kPinLed, LOW);
14      delay(200);
15    }
16    delay(1000); // 1 second
17  }
```

Listing C.5: solutions/Chap2_2/Chap2_2.pde

```
1   const int kPinLed = 2;
2
3   void setup()
4   {
5     pinMode(kPinLed, OUTPUT);
6   }
7
8   void loop()
9   {
10    for(int i = 0; i < 5; i++){
11      digitalWrite(kPinLed, HIGH);
12      delay(1000);
13      digitalWrite(kPinLed, LOW);
14      delay(1000);
15    }
```

```
16     for(int i = 0; i < 5; i++){
17       digitalWrite(kPinLed, HIGH);
18       delay(500);
19       digitalWrite(kPinLed, LOW);
20       delay(500);
21     }
22   }
```

Listing C.6: solutions/Chap2_3/Chap2_3.pde

```
1  const int k_numLEDs = 4;
2  const int kPinLeds[k_numLEDs] =  {2,3,4,5}; // LEDs connected↩
     ↪    to pins 2-5
3
4  void setup()
5  {
6    for(int i = 0; i < k_numLEDs; i++){
7      pinMode(kPinLeds[i], OUTPUT);
8    }
9  }
10
11 void loop()
12 {
13   for(int i = 0; i < k_numLEDs; i++){
14     digitalWrite(kPinLeds[i], HIGH);
15     delay(200);
16     digitalWrite(kPinLeds[i], LOW);
17   }
18   for(int i = k_numLEDs; i > 0; i--){
19     digitalWrite(kPinLeds[i - 1], HIGH);
20     delay(200);
21     digitalWrite(kPinLeds[i - 1], LOW);
22   }
23 }
```

## C.3 Chapter 3 Solutions

Listing C.7: solutions/Chap3_1/Chap3_1.pde

```
1   const int kPinButtonGas = 2;
2   const int kPinButtonBrake = 3;
3   const int kPinLed = 9;
4
5   void setup()
6   {
7     pinMode(kPinButtonGas, INPUT);
8     pinMode(kPinButtonBrake, INPUT);
9     pinMode(kPinLed, OUTPUT);
10    digitalWrite(kPinButtonGas, HIGH); // turn on pullup ↩
            ↪ resistor
11    digitalWrite(kPinButtonBrake, HIGH); // turn on pullup ↩
            ↪ resistor
12  }
13
14  int  delayTime = 500;
15  long lastTime = 0;
16  int ledState = LOW;
17  void loop()
18  {
19    if(digitalRead(kPinButtonGas) == LOW){
20      delayTime = delayTime--;
21    }
22    else if(digitalRead(kPinButtonBrake) == LOW){
23      delayTime = delayTime++;
24    }
25    delayTime = constrain(delayTime, 10, 5000);
26    if((lastTime + delayTime) < millis()){
27      ledState = !ledState;
28      digitalWrite(kPinLed, ledState);
29      lastTime = millis();
30    }
31    delay(10);
32  }
```

Listing C.8: solutions/Chap3_2/Chap3_2.pde

```
1   const int kPinPot = A0;
```

```
2   const int kPinButton = 2;
3   const int kPinLed = 9;
4
5   void setup()
6   {
7     pinMode(kPinLed, OUTPUT);
8     pinMode(kPinButton, INPUT);
9     digitalWrite(kPinButton, HIGH); // enable pull-up resistor
10  }
11
12  long int lastTime = 0;
13  int ledValue = LOW;
14  int sensorValue;
15
16  void loop()
17  {
18    if(digitalRead(kPinButton) == LOW){
19      sensorValue = analogRead(kPinPot);
20    }
21    if(millis() > lastTime + sensorValue){
22      if(ledValue == LOW){
23        ledValue = HIGH;
24      }
25      else{
26        ledValue = LOW;
27      }
28      lastTime = millis();
29      digitalWrite(kPinLed, ledValue);
30    }
31  }
```

Listing C.9: solutions/Chap3_3/Chap3_3.pde

```
1   const int kPinPot1 = A0;
2   const int kPinPot2 = A1;
3   const int kPinPot3 = A2;
4   const int kPinLed_R = 6;
5   const int kPinLed_G = 10;
6   const int kPinLed_B = 11;
```

```
7    const int kPinBtnTo = 2;
8    const int kPinBtnFrom = 3;
9
10   void setup()
11   {
12     pinMode(kPinLed_R, OUTPUT);
13     pinMode(kPinLed_G, OUTPUT);
14     pinMode(kPinLed_B, OUTPUT);
15     pinMode(kPinBtnTo, INPUT);
16     pinMode(kPinBtnFrom, INPUT);
17     digitalWrite(kPinBtnTo, HIGH);   // enable pull-up resistor
18     digitalWrite(kPinBtnFrom, HIGH); // enable pull-up resistor
19   }
20
21   int fromRed = 0;
22   int fromGreen = 0;
23   int fromBlue = 0;
24   int toRed = 255;
25   int toGreen = 255;
26   int toBlue = 255;
27
28   int currStep = 0;
29   int change = 1;
30
31   void loop()
32   {
33     int pot1Value;
34     int pot2Value;
35     int pot3Value;
36
37     pot1Value = analogRead(kPinPot1);
38     pot2Value = analogRead(kPinPot2);
39     pot3Value = analogRead(kPinPot3);
40
41     if(digitalRead(kPinBtnFrom) == LOW){
42       fromRed = map(pot1Value, 0, 1023, 0, 255);
43       analogWrite(kPinLed_R, fromRed);
44
45       fromGreen = map(pot2Value, 0, 1023, 0, 255);
```

136

```
46      analogWrite(kPinLed_R, fromGreen);
47
48      fromBlue = map(pot3Value, 0, 1023, 0, 255);
49      analogWrite(kPinLed_R, fromBlue);
50    }
51  else if(digitalRead(kPinBtnTo) == LOW){
52    toRed = map(pot1Value, 0, 1023, 0, 255);
53    analogWrite(kPinLed_R, toRed);
54
55    toGreen = map(pot2Value, 0, 1023, 0, 255);
56    analogWrite(kPinLed_G, toGreen);
57
58    toBlue = map(pot3Value, 0, 1023, 0, 255);
59    analogWrite(kPinLed_B, toBlue);
60  }
61  else{
62    currStep = currStep + change;
63    if(currStep > 255){
64      change = -1;
65      currStep = 255;
66    }
67    if(currStep < 0){
68      change = 1;
69      currStep = 0;
70    }
71
72    int ledValue = map(currStep, 0, 255, fromRed, toRed);
73    analogWrite(kPinLed_R, ledValue);
74
75    ledValue = map(currStep, 0, 255, fromGreen, toGreen);
76    analogWrite(kPinLed_G, ledValue);
77
78    ledValue = map(currStep, 0, 255, fromBlue, toBlue);
79    analogWrite(kPinLed_B, ledValue);
80    delay(4);  // because 4 * 255 = a litle more than 1000, 1↩
           ↪  second
81  }
82 }
```

## C.4  Chapter 4 Solutions

Listing C.10: solutions/Chap4_1/Chap4_1.pde

```
1  #include "pitches.h"
2
3  int speakerPin = 9;
4
5  #define NUM_NOTES 7
6
7  const int notes[NUM_NOTES] = // a 0 represents a rest
8  {
9    NOTE_C4, NOTE_C4, NOTE_D4, NOTE_C4,
10   NOTE_F4, NOTE_E4, 0
11 };
12
13 const int beats[NUM_NOTES] = {
14   1, 1, 2, 2, 2, 4, 4 };
15 const int tempo = 300;
16
17 void setup() {
18   pinMode(speakerPin, OUTPUT);
19 }
20
21 void loop() {
22   for (int i = 0; i < NUM_NOTES; i++) {
23     if (notes[i] == 0) {
24       delay(beats[i] * tempo); // rest
25     }
26     else {
27       ourTone(notes[i], beats[i] * tempo);
28     }
29     // pause between notes
30     delay(tempo / 2);
31   }
32 }
33
34 void ourTone(int freq, int duration)
35 {
```

```
36   tone(speakerPin, freq, duration);
37   delay(duration);
38   noTone(speakerPin);
39 }
```

Listing C.11: solutions/Chap4_2/Chap4_2.pde

```
1  #include "pitches.h"
2
3  const int k_speakerPin = 9;
4  const int k_btn1Pin = 2;
5  const int k_btn2Pin = 3;
6
7  #define NUM_NOTES_TUNE1 7
8
9  const int notes_tune1[NUM_NOTES_TUNE1] = // a 0 represents a ←
        ↪ rest
10 {
11   NOTE_C4, NOTE_C4, NOTE_D4, NOTE_C4,
12   NOTE_F4, NOTE_E4, 0
13 };
14
15 const int beats_tune1[NUM_NOTES_TUNE1] = {
16   1, 1, 2, 2, 2, 4, 4 };
17
18 #define NUM_NOTES_TUNE2 15
19
20 const int notes_tune2[NUM_NOTES_TUNE2] = // a 0 represents a ←
        ↪ rest
21 {
22   NOTE_C4, NOTE_C4, NOTE_G4, NOTE_G4,
23   NOTE_A4, NOTE_A4, NOTE_G4, NOTE_F4,
24   NOTE_F4, NOTE_E4, NOTE_E4, NOTE_D4,
25   NOTE_D4, NOTE_C4, 0
26 };
27
28 const int beats_tune2[NUM_NOTES_TUNE2] = {
29   1, 1, 1, 1, 1, 1, 2, 1, 1, 1, 1, 1, 1, 2, 4 };
30
```

```
31  const int tempo = 300;
32
33  void setup()
34  {
35    pinMode(k_speakerPin, OUTPUT);
36    pinMode(k_btn1Pin, INPUT);
37    pinMode(k_btn2Pin, INPUT);
38    digitalWrite(k_btn1Pin, HIGH); // turn on pull-up resistor
39    digitalWrite(k_btn2Pin, HIGH); // turn on pull-up resistor
40  }
41
42  void loop()
43  {
44    if(digitalRead(k_btn1Pin) == LOW){
45      playTune1();
46    }
47    if(digitalRead(k_btn2Pin) == LOW){
48      playTune2();
49    }
50  }
51
52  void playTune1()
53  {
54    for (int i = 0; i < NUM_NOTES_TUNE1; i++) {
55      if (notes_tune1[i] == 0) {
56        delay(beats_tune1[i] * tempo); // rest
57      }
58      else {
59        ourTone(notes_tune1[i], beats_tune1[i] * tempo);
60      }
61      // pause between notes
62      delay(tempo / 2);
63    }
64  }
65
66  void playTune2()
67  {
68    for (int i = 0; i < NUM_NOTES_TUNE2; i++) {
69      if (notes_tune2[i] == 0) {
```

```
70        delay(beats_tune2[i] * tempo); // rest
71      }
72      else {
73        ourTone(notes_tune2[i], beats_tune2[i] * tempo);
74      }
75      // pause between notes
76      delay(tempo / 2);
77    }
78  }
79
80  void ourTone(int freq, int duration)
81  {
82    tone(k_speakerPin, freq, duration);
83    delay(duration);
84    noTone(k_speakerPin);
85  }
```

Listing C.12: solutions/Chap4_3/Chap4_3.pde

```
1   #include "pitches.h"
2
3   const int k_speakerPin = 9;
4
5   #define NUM_NOTES 7
6
7   const int notes[NUM_NOTES] = // a 0 represents a rest
8   {
9     NOTE_C4, NOTE_C4, NOTE_D4, NOTE_C4,
10    NOTE_F4, NOTE_E4, 0
11  };
12
13  const int beats[NUM_NOTES] = {
14    1, 1, 2, 2, 2, 4, 4 };
15  const int tempo = 300;
16
17  void setup() {
18    pinMode(k_speakerPin, OUTPUT);
19  }
20
```

```
21  void loop() {
22    for (int i = 0; i < NUM_NOTES; i++) {
23      if (notes[i] == 0) {
24        delay(beats[i] * tempo); // rest
25      }
26      else {
27        ourTone(notes[i], beats[i] * tempo);
28      }
29      // pause between notes
30      delay(tempo / 2);
31    }
32  }
33
34  void ourTone(int freq, int duration)
35  {
36    long timeDelay = (1000000 / (2 * freq));  // calculate num ↩
          ↪ of microsec to delay
37    long endTime = millis() + duration;
38    // will have a bug with rollover time
39    while(millis() < endTime){
40      digitalWrite(k_speakerPin, HIGH);
41      delayMicroseconds(timeDelay);
42      digitalWrite(k_speakerPin, LOW);
43      delayMicroseconds(timeDelay);
44    }
45  }
```

## C.5  Chapter 5 Solutions

Listing C.13: solutions/Chap5_1/Chap5_1.pde

```
1  #include <PCD8544.h>
2
3  const int kPin_CLK = 5;
4  const int kPin_DIN = 6;
5  const int kPin_DC = 7;
6  const int kPin_RESET = 8;
```

```
7   const int kPin_Temp = A0;
8
9   PCD8544 lcd(kPin_CLK, kPin_DIN, kPin_DC, kPin_RESET);
10
11  void setup()
12  {
13    lcd.init();
14    lcd.setCursor(10,0);
15    lcd.print("Temperature:");
16  }
17
18  void loop()
19  {
20    float voltage = getVoltage();
21    float temperatureC = getTemperatureC(voltage);
22    // now convert to Fahrenheit
23    float temperatureF = convertToF(temperatureC);
24
25    lcd.setCursor(21,1);
26    lcd.print(temperatureC);
27    lcd.print(" C ");
28    lcd.setCursor(21,2);
29    lcd.print(temperatureF);
30    lcd.print(" F");
31    lcd.setCursor(21,3);
32    lcd.print(voltage);
33    lcd.print(" V");
34    delay(100);
35  }
36
37  float getVoltage()
38  {
39    int reading = analogRead(kPin_Temp);
40
41    return (reading * 5.0) / 1024;
42  }
43
44  float getTemperatureC(float voltage)
45  {
```

```
46    // convert from 10 mv per degree with 500mV offset
47    // to degrees ((voltage - 500mV) * 100)
48    return (voltage - 0.5) * 100;
49  }
50
51  float convertToF(float temperatureC)
52  {
53      return (temperatureC * 9.0 / 5.0) + 32.0;
54  }
```

Listing C.14: solutions/Chap5_2/Chap5_2.pde

```
1   #include <PCD8544.h>
2
3   const int kPin_CLK = 5;
4   const int kPin_DIN = 6;
5   const int kPin_DC = 7;
6   const int kPin_RESET = 8;
7   const int kPin_Temp = A0;
8
9   PCD8544 lcd(kPin_CLK, kPin_DIN, kPin_DC, kPin_RESET);
10
11  void setup()
12  {
13    lcd.init();
14    lcd.setCursor(10,0);
15    lcd.print("Temperature:");
16  }
17
18  float maxTemp = -200; // smaller than we can ever see
19  float minTemp = 200; // larger than we can ever see
20
21  void loop()
22  {
23    float temperatureC = getTemperatureC();
24     // now convert to Fahrenheit
25    float temperatureF = convertToF(temperatureC);
26
27    if(temperatureF > maxTemp){
```

```
28      maxTemp = temperatureF;
29    }
30    if(temperatureF < minTemp){
31      minTemp = temperatureF;
32    }
33
34    lcd.setCursor(16,1);
35    lcd.print(temperatureF);
36    lcd.print(" F");
37    lcd.setCursor(16, 2);
38    lcd.print(maxTemp);
39    lcd.print(" F max");
40    lcd.setCursor(16, 3);
41    lcd.print(minTemp);
42    lcd.print(" F min");
43    delay(100);
44 }
45
46 float getTemperatureC()
47 {
48    int reading = analogRead(kPin_Temp);
49
50    float voltage = (reading * 5.0) / 1024;
51    // convert from 10 mv per degree with 500mV offset
52    // to degrees ((voltage - 500mV) * 100)
53    return (voltage - 0.5) * 100;
54 }
55
56 float convertToF(float temperatureC)
57 {
58      return (temperatureC * 9.0 / 5.0) + 32.0;
59 }
```

Listing C.15: solutions/Chap5_3/Chap5_3.pde

```
1 #include <PCD8544.h>
2
3 const int kPin_CLK = 5;
4 const int kPin_DIN = 6;
```

```
5  const int kPin_DC = 7;
6  const int kPin_RESET = 8;
7  const int kPin_Temp = A0;
8
9  PCD8544 lcd(kPin_CLK, kPin_DIN, kPin_DC, kPin_RESET);
10
11 void setup()
12 {
13   lcd.init();
14   lcd.setCursor(10,0);
15   lcd.print("Temperature:");
16 }
17
18 float maxTemp = -200; // smaller than we can ever see
19 long maxTime;
20 float minTemp = 200; // larger than we can ever see
21 long minTime;
22
23 void loop()
24 {
25   float temperatureC = getTemperatureC();
26    // now convert to Fahrenheit
27   float temperatureF = convertToF(temperatureC);
28
29   if(temperatureF > maxTemp){
30     maxTemp = temperatureF;
31     maxTime = millis();
32   }
33   if(temperatureF < minTemp){
34     minTemp = temperatureF;
35     minTime = millis();
36   }
37
38   lcd.setCursor(21,1);
39   lcd.print(temperatureF);
40   lcd.print(" F");
41   lcd.setCursor(0, 2);
42   lcd.print(maxTemp);
43   lcd.print(" F max");
```

146

```
44     lcd.setCursor(0,3);
45     lcd.print((millis() - maxTime) / 1000);
46     lcd.print(" secs ago");
47     lcd.setCursor(0, 4);
48     lcd.print(minTemp);
49     lcd.print(" F min");
50     lcd.setCursor(0,5);
51     lcd.print((millis() - minTime) / 1000);
52     lcd.print(" secs ago");
53
54     delay(100);
55  }
56
57  float getTemperatureC()
58  {
59     int reading = analogRead(kPin_Temp);
60
61     float voltage = (reading * 5.0) / 1024;
62     // convert from 10 mv per degree with 500mV offset
63     // to degrees ((voltage - 500mV) * 100)
64     return (voltage - 0.5) * 100;
65  }
66
67  float convertToF(float temperatureC)
68  {
69        return (temperatureC * 9.0 / 5.0) + 32.0;
70  }
```

## C.6  Chapter 6 Solutions

Listing C.16: solutions/Chap6_1/Chap6_1.pde

```
1  #include <PCD8544.h>
2
3  const int kPin_Btn = 2;
4  const int kPin_SCLK = 5;
5  const int kPin_SDIN = 6;
```

```
 6  const int kPin_DC = 7;
 7  const int kPin_RESET = 8;
 8  const int kPin_Temp = A0;
 9
10  PCD8544 lcd(kPin_SCLK, kPin_SDIN, kPin_DC, kPin_RESET);
11
12  // A bitmap graphic (5x1) of a degree symbol
13  const int DEGREE_WIDTH = 5;
14  const int DEGREE_HEIGHT = 1;
15  const byte degreesBitmap[] = { 0x00, 0x07, 0x05, 0x07, 0x00 ←↩
        ↪ };
16
17  // A bitmap graphic (10x2) of a thermometer...
18  const int THERMO_WIDTH = 10;
19  const int THERMO_HEIGHT = 2;
20  const byte thermometerBitmap[] =
21  { 0x00, 0x00, 0x48, 0xfe, 0x01, 0xfe, 0x00, 0x02, 0x05, 0x02,
22    0x00, 0x00, 0x62, 0xff, 0xfe, 0xff, 0x60, 0x00, 0x00, 0x00←↩
          ↪ };
23
24  const int LCD_WIDTH = 84;
25  const int LCD_HEIGHT = 6;
26  const int GRAPH_HEIGHT = 5;
27
28  const int MIN_TEMP = 50;
29  const int MAX_TEMP = 100;
30
31  void setup()
32  {
33    pinMode(kPin_Btn, INPUT);
34    digitalWrite(kPin_Btn, HIGH);   // turn on pull-up resistor
35    lcd.init();
36    lcd.setCursor(10,0);
37    lcd.print("Temperature:");
38    lcd.setCursor(0, LCD_HEIGHT - THERMO_HEIGHT);
39    lcd.drawBitmap(thermometerBitmap, THERMO_WIDTH, ←↩
          ↪ THERMO_HEIGHT);
40  }
41
```

```
42   int xChart = LCD_WIDTH;
43
44   void loop()
45   {
46     float temperatureC = getTemperatureC();
47     // now convert to Fahrenheit
48     float temperatureF = convertToF(temperatureC);
49
50     if(digitalRead(kPin_Btn) == LOW){
51       xChart = THERMO_WIDTH + 2;
52       lcd.setCursor(xChart, 2);
53       // clear it
54       while(xChart <= LCD_WIDTH){
55         drawColumn(0);
56         xChart++;
57       }
58       xChart = THERMO_WIDTH + 2;
59     }
60
61     lcd.setCursor(21,1);
62     lcd.print(temperatureF);
63     lcd.drawBitmap(degreesBitmap, DEGREE_WIDTH, DEGREE_HEIGHT);
64     lcd.print(" F");
65     if(xChart >= LCD_WIDTH){
66       xChart = THERMO_WIDTH + 2;
67     }
68     lcd.setCursor(xChart, 2);
69     int dataHeight = map(temperatureF, MIN_TEMP, MAX_TEMP, 0, ←
           ↪ GRAPH_HEIGHT * 8);
70
71     drawColumn(dataHeight);
72     drawColumn(0);   // marker to see current chart position
73     xChart++;
74
75     delay(500);
76   }
77
78   float getTemperatureC()
79   {
```

```
80    int reading = analogRead(kPin_Temp);
81
82    float voltage = (reading * 5.0) / 1024;
83    // convert from 10 mv per degree with 500mV offset
84    // to degrees ((voltage - 500mV) * 100)
85    return (voltage - 0.5) * 100;
86  }
87
88  float convertToF(float temperatureC)
89  {
90      return (temperatureC * 9.0 / 5.0) + 32.0;
91  }
92
93  const byte dataBitmap[] =
94  {0x00, 0x80, 0xC0, 0xE0, 0xF0, 0xF8, 0xFC, 0xFE};
95
96  void drawColumn(unsigned int value)
97  {
98      byte graphBitmap[GRAPH_HEIGHT];
99      int i;
100
101     if(value > (GRAPH_HEIGHT * 8)){
102       value = GRAPH_HEIGHT * 8;
103     }
104     // value is number of pixels to draw
105
106     //1. clear all pixels in graphBitmap
107     for(i = 0; i < GRAPH_HEIGHT; i++){
108       graphBitmap[i] = 0x00;
109     }
110
111     //2. Fill all of the ones that should be completely full
112     i = 0;
113     while(value >= 8){
114         graphBitmap[GRAPH_HEIGHT - 1 - i] = 0xFF;
115         value -= 8;
116         i++;
117     }
118     if(i != GRAPH_HEIGHT){
```

```
119        graphBitmap[GRAPH_HEIGHT - 1 - i] = dataBitmap[value];
120      }
121      lcd.drawBitmap(graphBitmap, 1, GRAPH_HEIGHT);
122    }
```

Listing C.17: solutions/Chap6_2/Chap6_2.pde

```
1   #include <PCD8544.h>
2
3   const int kPin_Btn = 2;
4   const int kPin_SCLK = 5;
5   const int kPin_SDIN = 6;
6   const int kPin_DC = 7;
7   const int kPin_RESET = 8;
8   const int kPin_Temp = A0;
9
10  PCD8544 lcd(kPin_SCLK, kPin_SDIN, kPin_DC, kPin_RESET);
11
12  // A bitmap graphic (5x1) of a degree symbol
13  const int DEGREE_WIDTH = 5;
14  const int DEGREE_HEIGHT = 1;
15  const byte degreesBitmap[] = { 0x00, 0x07, 0x05, 0x07, 0x00 ↩
        ↪ };
16
17  // A bitmap graphic (10x2) of a thermometer...
18  const int THERMO_WIDTH = 10;
19  const int THERMO_HEIGHT = 2;
20  const byte thermometerBitmap[] =
21  { 0x00, 0x00, 0x48, 0xfe, 0x01, 0xfe, 0x00, 0x02, 0x05, 0x02,
22    0x00, 0x00, 0x62, 0xff, 0xfe, 0xff, 0x60, 0x00, 0x00, 0x00↩
        ↪ };
23
24  const int LCD_WIDTH = 84;
25  const int LCD_HEIGHT = 6;
26  const int GRAPH_HEIGHT = 5;
27
28  const int MIN_TEMP = 50;
29  const int MAX_TEMP = 100;
30
```

```
31  void setup()
32  {
33    pinMode(kPin_Btn, INPUT);
34    digitalWrite(kPin_Btn, HIGH);   // turn on pull-up resistor
35    lcd.init();
36    lcd.setCursor(10,0);
37    lcd.print("Temperature:");
38    lcd.setCursor(0, LCD_HEIGHT - THERMO_HEIGHT);
39    lcd.drawBitmap(thermometerBitmap, THERMO_WIDTH, ←
          ↪ THERMO_HEIGHT);
40  }
41
42  int xChart = LCD_WIDTH;
43  bool displayF = true;
44
45  void loop()
46  {
47    float temperatureC = getTemperatureC();
48     // now convert to Fahrenheit
49    float temperatureF = convertToF(temperatureC);
50
51    if(digitalRead(kPin_Btn) == LOW){
52      displayF = !displayF;
53      while(digitalRead(kPin_Btn) == LOW){
54      }
55    }
56
57    lcd.setCursor(21,1);
58    if(displayF){
59        lcd.print(temperatureF);
60    }
61    else{
62      lcd.print(temperatureC);
63    }
64    lcd.drawBitmap(degreesBitmap, DEGREE_WIDTH, DEGREE_HEIGHT);
65    if(displayF){
66        lcd.print(" F");
67    }
68    else{
```

152

```
69     lcd.print(" C");
70   }
71   if(xChart >= LCD_WIDTH){
72     xChart = THERMO_WIDTH + 2;
73   }
74   lcd.setCursor(xChart, 2);
75   int dataHeight = map(temperatureF, MIN_TEMP, MAX_TEMP, 0, ←
           ↪ GRAPH_HEIGHT * 8);
76
77   drawColumn(dataHeight);
78   drawColumn(0);   // marker to see current chart position
79   xChart++;
80
81   delay(500);
82 }
83
84 float getTemperatureC()
85 {
86   int reading = analogRead(kPin_Temp);
87
88   float voltage = (reading * 5.0) / 1024;
89   // convert from 10 mv per degree with 500mV offset
90   // to degrees ((voltage - 500mV) * 100)
91   return (voltage - 0.5) * 100;
92 }
93
94 float convertToF(float temperatureC)
95 {
96     return (temperatureC * 9.0 / 5.0) + 32.0;
97 }
98
99 const byte dataBitmap[] =
100 {0x00, 0x80, 0xC0, 0xE0, 0xF0, 0xF8, 0xFC, 0xFE};
101
102 void drawColumn(unsigned int value)
103 {
104     byte graphBitmap[GRAPH_HEIGHT];
105     int i;
106
```

```
107    if(value > (GRAPH_HEIGHT * 8)){
108      value = GRAPH_HEIGHT * 8;
109    }
110    // value is number of pixels to draw
111
112    //1. clear all pixels in graphBitmap
113    for(i = 0; i < GRAPH_HEIGHT; i++){
114      graphBitmap[i] = 0x00;
115    }
116
117    //2. Fill all of the ones that should be completely full
118    i = 0;
119    while(value >= 8){
120        graphBitmap[GRAPH_HEIGHT - 1 - i] = 0xFF;
121        value -= 8;
122        i++;
123    }
124    if(i != GRAPH_HEIGHT){
125        graphBitmap[GRAPH_HEIGHT - 1 - i] = dataBitmap[value];
126    }
127    lcd.drawBitmap(graphBitmap, 1, GRAPH_HEIGHT);
128 }
```

## C.7  Chapter 7 Solutions

Listing C.18: solutions/Chap7_1/Chap7_1.pde

```
1  const int kPin_LED = 9;
2  const int kPin_Photocell = A1;
3
4  void setup()
5  {
6    pinMode(kPin_LED, OUTPUT);
7  }
8
9  void loop()
10 {
```

154

```
11    int value = analogRead(kPin_Photocell);
12    int brightness = map(value, 0, 1023, 0, 255);
13
14    analogWrite(kPin_LED, brightness);
15  }
```

Listing C.19: solutions/Chap7_2/Chap7_2.pde

```
1  const int kPin_Tilt = 3;
2  const int kPin_LED  = 13;
3  const int kPin_Speaker = 9;
4
5  void setup()
6  {
7    pinMode(kPin_Tilt, INPUT);
8    digitalWrite(kPin_Tilt, HIGH);  // turn on built-in pull-up↩
           ↪  resistor
9    pinMode(kPin_LED, OUTPUT);
10   pinMode(kPin_Speaker, OUTPUT);
11 }
12
13 void loop()
14 {
15   if(digitalRead(kPin_Tilt) == LOW){
16     digitalWrite(kPin_LED, HIGH);
17     soundAlarm();
18   }
19   else{
20     digitalWrite(kPin_LED, LOW);
21   }
22 }
23
24 void soundAlarm()
25 {
26   for(int freq = 440; freq < 4000; freq = freq * 2){
27     tone(9, 440);
28     delay(10);
29   }
30   noTone(9);
```

```
31  }
```

Listing C.20: solutions/Chap7_3/Chap7_3.pde

```
1   const int k_ReedSwitchPin = 2;
2   const int k_Pin_Speaker = 9;
3   const int k_LEDPin = 13;
4
5   void setup()
6   {
7     pinMode(k_ReedSwitchPin, INPUT);
8     digitalWrite(k_ReedSwitchPin, HIGH); // turn on pullup ↩
        ↪ resistor
9     pinMode(k_LEDPin, OUTPUT);
10    pinMode(k_Pin_Speaker, OUTPUT);
11  }
12
13  void loop()
14  {
15    if(digitalRead(k_ReedSwitchPin) == LOW){
16      digitalWrite(k_LEDPin, HIGH);
17      tone(k_Pin_Speaker, 440);
18    }
19    else{
20      digitalWrite(k_LEDPin, LOW);
21      noTone(k_Pin_Speaker);
22    }
23  }
```

Listing C.21: solutions/Chap7_4/Chap7_4.pde

```
1   #include "pitches.h"
2
3   const int k_speakerPin = 9;
4   const int k_sensorPin = A5;
5   const int k_threshold = 100;
6
7   #define NUM_NOTES 15
8
```

156

```
 9  const int notes[NUM_NOTES] = // a 0 represents a rest
10  {
11    NOTE_C4, NOTE_C4, NOTE_G4, NOTE_G4,
12    NOTE_A4, NOTE_A4, NOTE_G4, NOTE_F4,
13    NOTE_F4, NOTE_E4, NOTE_E4, NOTE_D4,
14    NOTE_D4, NOTE_C4, 0
15  };
16
17  const int beats[NUM_NOTES] = {
18    1, 1, 1, 1, 1, 1, 2, 1, 1, 1, 1, 1, 1, 2, 4 };
19  const int tempo = 300;
20
21  void setup()
22  {
23    pinMode(k_speakerPin, OUTPUT);
24  }
25
26  void loop()
27  {
28    if (analogRead(k_sensorPin) >= k_threshold) {
29      playTune();
30    }
31  }
32
33  void playTune()
34  {
35    for (int i = 0; i < NUM_NOTES; i++) {
36      if (notes[i] == 0) {
37        delay(beats[i] * tempo); // rest
38      }
39      else {
40        ourTone(notes[i], beats[i] * tempo);
41      }
42      // pause between notes
43      delay(tempo / 2);
44    }
45  }
46
47
```

```
48
49   void ourTone(int freq, int duration)
50   {
51     tone(k_speakerPin, freq, duration);
52     delay(duration);
53     noTone(k_speakerPin);
54   }
```

## C.8 Chapter 8 Solutions

Listing C.22: solutions/Chap8_1/Chap8_1.pde

```
1    const int k_JoystickX_Pin = A5;
2    const int k_JoystickY_Pin = A4;
3    const int k_Joystick_Fire = 2;
4
5    const int k_ledUP_Pin = 3;
6    const int k_ledDOWN_Pin = 4;
7    const int k_ledLEFT_Pin = 5;
8    const int k_ledRIGHT_Pin = 6;
9    const int k_ledFIRE_Pin = 7;
10
11   const int JOYX_LEFT = 300;
12   const int JOYX_RIGHT = 700;
13   const int JOYY_UP = 700;
14   const int JOYY_DOWN = 300;
15
16   void setup()
17   {
18     pinMode(k_Joystick_Fire, INPUT);
19     digitalWrite(k_Joystick_Fire, HIGH);   // turn on pull-up ↩
           ↪ resistor
20     pinMode(k_ledUP_Pin, OUTPUT);
21     pinMode(k_ledDOWN_Pin, OUTPUT);
22     pinMode(k_ledLEFT_Pin, OUTPUT);
23     pinMode(k_ledRIGHT_Pin, OUTPUT);
24     pinMode(k_ledFIRE_Pin, OUTPUT);
```

```
25  }
26
27  void loop()
28  {
29    int xVal = analogRead(k_JoystickX_Pin);
30    int yVal = analogRead(k_JoystickY_Pin);
31
32    int left = false;
33    int right = false;
34    int up = false;
35    int down = false;
36    int fire = false;
37
38    if(xVal < JOYX_LEFT){
39     left = true;
40    }
41    else if(xVal > JOYX_RIGHT){
42      right = true;
43    }
44    if(yVal < JOYY_DOWN){
45      down = true;
46    }
47    else if(yVal > JOYY_UP){
48      up = true;
49    }
50    if(digitalRead(k_Joystick_Fire) == LOW){
51      fire = true;
52    }
53    digitalWrite(k_ledUP_Pin, up);
54    digitalWrite(k_ledDOWN_Pin, down);
55    digitalWrite(k_ledLEFT_Pin, left);
56    digitalWrite(k_ledRIGHT_Pin, right);
57    digitalWrite(k_ledFIRE_Pin, fire);
58  }
```

Listing C.23: solutions/Chap8_2/Chap8_2.pde

```
1  #include <Servo.h>
2
```

```
3    const int k_Servo_Pin = 9;
4
5    Servo servo;
6
7    void setup()
8    {
9      servo.attach(k_Servo_Pin);
10   }
11
12   void loop()
13   {
14     for(int i = 0; i < 180; i++){
15       servo.write(i);
16       delay(20);
17     }
18     for(int i = 180; i > 0; i--){
19       servo.write(i);
20       delay(20);
21     }
22   }
```